34 MEN

A Study of the men of Moulton village
who died serving humanity
in the Great War 1914–1918.

Compiled and written
by Geoff Crompton

Designed and edited
by Ted Smith

In Gratitude

34 Men of Moulton lie in graves
Beneath the changing sky
They gave their youth that we might see
Our lives through......to eternity.

We clasp their hands across the void
Salute them through our tears of pride
And pray to God that never again
Will our young men endure such pain.

GAC

First published in 2001 by
IMCC Ltd
Riverdream
Taggs Island, Hampton TW12 2HA

Content © Geoffrey A Crompton
Introduction © Tony Spagnoly
Front Cover design © Ted Smith

A CIP catalogue record for this book is available
from the British Library
ISBN Number 1-902185-09-9

Edited and Designed by Ted Smith
Typeset by IMCC Ltd. in ITC Garamond

Printed by Wonder Works
16a Pepper Street
Nantwich
Cheshire CW5 5AB

FOREWORD

President Abraham Lincoln said some potent words about 'remembrance' after 'Gettysburg' in 1865, the defining battle of the American Civil War. He said:

Why do we need to remember? Sacrifice is quite meaningless without remembrance! Too often as a nation, we take for granted the freedom we cherish today. Freedoms purchased with the blood and sacrifice of others! That is why we need to remember!

The great man was quite right of course. Too often in recent years, during this quite amazing explosion of interest in all things 1914–1918, we pass the many war memorials of all sizes throughout the country, look at the names carved there in a quite casual way, and then go on our journey. And yet, if we stand and ponder for a moment, the sensitive soul will take on board the theme of remembrance that Abraham Lincoln was propounding, and understood.

A E Houseman, the great English writer, once said, when referring to the nation's fallen:

Here dead we lie, because we did not choose to live and shame the land from which we sprung. Life to be sure is nothing much to lose, but young men think it is, and we were young!

At least, thanks to Geoff Crompton and this splendidly memorable book detailing their collective sacrifice, the young men of Moulton who fell in the Great War will have nothing to feel shame for. Geoff records their lives where possible, their military service, and supplies a picture where available.

These village men, everyone a son, a brother or a husband, some with relatives living today, are buried at home, on the old British Western Front or even further afield. They will never again be just bland names carved in stone, for Geoff with his inquisitive, sensitive spirit has ensured that they will live amongst us 'for evermore', and be remembered with pride.

This book records their passing in a human way, and is an enduring tribute to young men long gone from our sight.

May they all rest in peace.

My son died by the hand of strangers,
But by a strangers hand, his limbs were reposed
(Inscription on the headstone of a British soldier at Ypres)

Tony Spagnoly, October 2001

INTRODUCTION

On a Sunday night in the late autumn of 1998, my wife Lois and I were attending evensong at St. Stephen's Parish Church in Moulton. We occupied a pew on the right of the aisle and directly in front of a green marble memorial tablet commemorating those men of the village who had given their lives in the Great War of 1914–1918.

I began to read through the names of the 34 men listed, and noted that some surnames repeated themselves – four Buckley's, two Clarkes and three Tomlinsons. My mind began to wander and, with no disrespect to Stephen Wilson our vicar, or his sermon for that matter, I began to wonder about these men of yesteryear. Who were they? Where did they live? What did they do for a living? Were any of them related? How did they die and where? Did anyone know? Did anyone care?

I resolved then and there that I would conduct a study of each and every one of those men and to write something about them for posterity.

In the research and preparation of this tribute I have tried to ensure that all detail is correct. My greatest stumbling block however, has been the non-availability of a confirmed list of regimental numbers for them. They are not to be found in any archive I have searched and, in one or two cases, I have had to make considered guesses on certain data. If I have guessed incorrectly, I apologise.

What follows then is my amateurish attempt to do justice to the memory of those men and, at the same time, to record my own appreciation for what they sacrificed for me.

Geoff Crompton, October 2001

ACKNOWLEDGEMENTS

It would have been extremely difficult, if not impossible, to have put this tribute together without the help, support and understanding of countless numbers of people and organisations, some of whom are listed below:

Relatives of the 34 men; The Villagers of Moulton; Moulton Village News, BACSA; Librarians at Northwich and Winsford; Staff at The Northwich Salt Museum; Archivists at Cheshire Records Office; The Editors of the Northwich/ Winsford Guardians and Northwich Chronicle for allowing the publication of photographs; Plymouth City Museum & Art Gallery collection; Roy Westlake for the use of his line drawings of Regimental badges; The Imperial War Museum, London for allowing free use of Crown Copyright photographs; Andrew Naden for his permission to print his poem *A Last Bombardment*; The Reverend Stephen Wilson for the photograph of the Memorial East Window in St. Stephens Church; Brunner Mond Ltd for the use of photographs of their memorials; The Regimental Records Officers of the Regiments in which the 34 men served, and for their help and advice on Regimental war diaries, histories, photographs and badge illustrations; Stephen Barker for permission to use extracts from his article for the Western Front Association about three Northwich soldiers; Kim Clarke, of the Commonwealth War Graves Commission for photographs of the two graves in Greece; Earl Bateman for information on production at Brunner Mond's Lostock Works during the Great War; Alan Ravenscroft, for his photographs of Winsford and Whitegate War Memorials; Peter and Paul Nixon for the photograph of Vis-en-Artois Memorial; Joy Bratherton of The South Cheshire branch, Western Front Asociation; Ian Alexander, of the War Research Society for providing many of the grave photographs and for sharing some of his vast knowledge with me; David Coulbeck, Headmaster of Moulton County Primary School, for the loan of old school photographs; Tony Spagnoly, Military Author and Researcher for casting his experienced eye over my amateur efforts and for his Foreword; Ted Smith for the design of the front cover, for the supply of mny of the photographs and for putting the book into such perfect order. My friends Donald Crawford and Phil Ashton, for their suggestions, encouragement and help, and Les Burgess for listening patiently each Thursday evening over our weekly pint in the Moulton British Legion, whilst I recounted my latest 'find'; Grant Stanning, my son-in-law, for proof reading the finished manuscript; to Lois, my wife, for tolerating my long hours away from home and the time spent in my 'eyrie' putting this tribute together; And finally, to all those unnamed friends and acquaintances who listened, helped, provided and encouraged.

Geoff Crompton, October 2001

CONTENTS

A Last Bombardment
As we sit here in our trench,
Amidst the mud – the blood – the stench,
I can't think straight but wonder why
How and when we all shall die.

The thunder never goes away –
Shell after shell – day after day –
The earth heaves up to rain back down.
We cling to life in our piece of ground.

Night gives way to another dawn,
To the warmth of the sun on a bright new morn.
Once again the shells we hear,
To fill us again with an endless fear.

A flash – a bang – a cannon's roar
Oh god we are gone – we are no more!!
For now I am in my endless sleep
Will you for ever my memory keep?

For in this foreign field we lie
With fine white stone to remember by.
So when at last you come to see
All my fine mates who lie with me.

These fields where the poppies grow
   – each one a soul of us you know!
To sway to and fro but never bend
   – just like the British soldier to the end.

Andrew Naden, September 2001
In memory of his grandfather,
Private. David Naden,
killed on the Somme, 1916

The 34 Men

Sam Ashley
Fred J Bates
Alfred Barber
Ernest Blythe
Arnold Buckley
Robert H Buckley
Robert Buckley
Wilmot Buckley
Jervis Clarke
William J Clarke
William H Cookson
John Crank
Walter Didsbury
John William Foster
George Greatbanks
Harry Groves
Horace Hitchinson

Harry Hodkinson
John William Jones
Jack Maddock
Oliver Middleton
Arthur Noden
George Ravenscroft
Joseph Shaw
James Southern
Thomas Southern
Dan Tomlinson
Enoch Tomlinson
John Tomlinson
Peter Wakefield
Albert V Walker
George Weedon
Arthur F Wilkinson
Joseph Yardley

Dedicated to the Glory of God and in Loving Memory of
the men of Moulton Parish who gave their lives in the
Great War 1914–1918

The Moulton Village War Memorial

The War Memorial

O N 25 APRIL 1919 a public meeting was held in the Moulton village Verdin Institute to consider the question of a memorial to the lads of the village who had given their lives during the struggle. The Reverend J T Vale presided. It was agreed that a committee be formed to raise funds by public subscription for a stone monument bearing the names of those who had fallen. This to be erected on a suitable site close to the heart of the village. It was estimated that a sum of £350 would be required to complete the work and that £40 had already been subscribed.

By 19 August 1919, the design and site for the memorial was agreed. It would take the form of a soldier of the Cheshires, with rifle 'at ease', set on a raised plinth of Yorkshire stone. The figure would be sculpted in Italian marble by Mr Samuel Welsby, of Mossley Hill and Widnes. The names of the 34 men would be deeply inscribed on the face and infilled with lead. Salt Union Ltd, having been approached, donated a plot of land at the side of Main Road and more or less opposite the lower entrance to Regent Street. The Subscription Fund was growing, but slowly. It was hoped that the final sum would be reached in the last quarter of 1919.

On Saturday 18 December 1920, a large gathering of villagers and their guests formed a procession at the Verdin Institute. Headed by the village band, under the direction of Mr Hitchinson, the procession paraded the village before halting at the memorial. Members of the Hartford Church Lads Brigade formed the Guard of Honour. Many ex-servicemen were present to pay their respects to those of their fallen comrades who didn't make it home. There were signs of deep mourning as Reverend J T Vale read out the names of the fallen. After hymns, led by the Memorial Choir, Captain W H France-Hayhurst gave the address. He went on to say that he could do no better than to quote the words of the King written on the scrolls presented to the next of kin "See to it that their names are not forgotten". The unveiling service ended with the sounding of *Reveille*.

The East Window in St. Stephen's Church, Moulton

The East Window

A T A MEETING of the Parochial Church Council in April 1920 it was suggested that a Parish Church War Memorial be placed on the agenda for discussion at some later date.

On 10 October 1921 a decision was taken to place an East Window and Tablet in St. Stephen's Church in memory of all men of Moulton who had died in the Great War. The estimated cost of £300 was to be raised by donations, summer sales and the like. A figure of £73 was already held towards this sum.

By May 1922 the fund had swelled to £128, with the estimate for the work quoted at £320. In October 1922 the Diocesan Registry at Chester granted a Faculty for the East Window Memorial. By early 1923, the majority of the money had been raised, and work began. The East Window was designed by John Bewsey RA and the following inscription agreed upon:

> Remember O Lord with compassion thy servants who, going forth from this Parish, gave their lives for their King and Country in the Great War 1914 – 1918

4 February 1923 was designated for the unveiling and dedication of the new window. At 2.15 pm the parade assembled at the Beehive corner under the command of Sergeant Major Oakes. It then proceeded to the church were a service of dedication took place. After Captain France-Hayhurst J.P. had unveiled the window, the Lord Bishop of Chester performed the dedication ceremony.

THE EAST WINDOW
AND THIS TABLET ARE DEDICATED
TO THE GLORY OF GOD
AND IN
GRATEFUL AND LOVING MEMORY
OF THE MEN OF THIS PARISH
WHO GAVE THEIR LIVES IN THE
GREAT WAR 1914-1918.

SAM ASHLEY	HARRY HODKINSON
FRED JAMES BATES	JOHN WILLIAM JONES
ALFRED BARBER	JACK MADDOCK
ERNEST BLYTHE	OLIVER MIDDLETON
ARNOLD BUCKLEY	ARTHUR NODEN
ROBERT H. BUCKLEY	GEORGE RAVENSCROFT
ROBERT BUCKLEY	JOSEPH SHAW
WILMOT BUCKLEY	JAMES SOUTHERN
JERVIS CLARKE	THOMAS SOUTHERN
WILLIAM J. CLARKE	DAN TOMLINSON
WILLIAM H. COOKSON	ENOCH TOMLINSON
JOHN CRANK	JOHN TOMLINSON
WALTER DIDSBURY	PETER WAKEFIELD
JOHN WILLIAM FOSTER	ALBERT VICTOR WALKER
GEORGE GREATBANKS	GEORGE WEEDON
HARRY GROVES	ARTHUR F. WILKINSON
HORACE HUTCHINSON	JOSEPH YARDLEY

"MAKE THEM TO BE NUMBERED WITH
THY SAINTS IN GLORY EVERLASTING."

The wall Tablet and Shelf in St. Stephen's Church, Moulton

The Tablet and Shelf

A S A FINAL ACT of remembrance the congregation of St. Stephens made a decision in July 1923 to place within their Church a suitable Tablet and Shelf on which would be listed the names of the 34 men of the Village who had laid down their lives. A faculty was granted by the Diocesan Registry at Chester on 18 September 1923. All was now set for the work to begin.

By October it was agreed that green marble and alabaster would be used for the construction. At the same time a suitable inscription was agreed.

On Sunday 18 November 1923 at 3.0 pm, and to a packed church, the unveiling and dedication of the Tablet and Shelf was performed by the Reverend Canon Sanders of Davenham. The service was conducted by Reverend J T Vale.

Regent Street, Moulton, with he war memorial sited at the far end

The Village

M OULTON VILLAGE stands in the heart of the Cheshire countryside between the towns of Northwich and Winsford. Located on a ridge overlooking the vale, it runs more or less parallel with the River Weaver. The 1086 Domesday Book mentions that 'Moletune' was part of the estate of The Baron Richard de Vernon of Shipbrook. Roughly translated from the old English the entry reads:

> Moulton. Leofnorth held it – he was a freeman. There is one hide paying tax.
> There is land for 2 ploughs.
> There is one villager and one smallholder who have 1/2 plough.
> There is 1 acre of meadow; Woodland 1 league long and 1 wide; 1 enclosure.
> Value was and is 5s (25p).

In the mid-18th century, Moulton and the surrounding area was purchased by the France-Hayhurst family who took up residence in nearby Bostock Hall. The estate was sold during the 1950s. Bostock Hall was converted into flats in the late 90s. Today the village boasts two places of worship: The Methodist Chapel, dating from 1875, and The Parish Church of St Stephen the Martyr, built in 1876. It has two pubs: The Lion and The Travellers Rest, a County Primary School built in 1894, a Village Hall, British Legion Club, Verdin Institute and Youth Group Headquarters.

In 1801, the population of the village was 103. In 1851 it had risen to 328, in 1901 to 1,004, in 1951 to 1,218 and, in 1997, to 2,330. In this current year (2001) the figure exceeds 3,000. The heart of the old village, comprising Main Road, Regent Street, Church Street, Chapel Lane and Chapel Street is now surrounded by new estates of houses, bungalows and flats.

Employment in the 19th and early 20th century was dominated by the salt industry, and the houses in Regent Street and Church Street were built to house its workers. At dawn, salt workers would trudge up the rise from their homes, then down the path past the Sand Pit and under the railway tunnels to the Newbridge Salt Works. Some would walk further, crossing the River Weaver to clock-on at Falk's Salt Works. When Sir John

Attendees of the village school in the early 1920s

Brunner and Ludwig Mond established their Chemical Plants in Northwich towards the end of the 19th century, men from Moulton sought jobs in their factories at Winnington and Lostock.

Life in Moulton prior to 1914 was typical of a country village in the early part of the 20th century. Men worked on the land and at various trades in and beyond the village. Their wives brought up large families in small houses, with three children to a bed not being uncommon. The 1891 Census repeatedly lists the occupation of the head of the household as Salt Boiler, the job being to look after large open pans filled with salt brine. The Salt Boiler tended the fires under the pans and regulated the flow of brine into them until a combination of time and heat produced the required crystal size. Various grades of salt from 'bock' through to very fine granular were made. The process could take up to a week after which time the pans would be emptied, cleaned and the cycle repeated. It was hot, steamy, sweaty and intensive labour with the men stripped to the waist and wearing clogs to keep their feet dry.

The village war memorial stands on the side of Main Road on land donated by The Salt Union Ltd. The figure of the soldier faces Regent Street surveying the houses from which many of the 34 men made their last journey. The memorial was vandalised by mindless idiots in 1998 but has now been fully restored.

A Salt Boiler tending his pans

Death has no Favourites

A SURVIVOR OF THE Great War whose name is etched on the memorial close to those of the 34 men, was Captain W H France-Hayhurst, Lord of the Manor of Bostock and Davenham, who lived at Bostock Hall. He was the third son of Colonel Charles Hoskin France-Hayhurst whose family took over the estate, including most of the village, from the heirs of Thomas Cholmondeley, in the 18th Century. The France-Hayhursts continued to run the estate until its sale in the 1950s. It was Captain France-Hayhurst who unveiled the memorial on 18 December 1920.

The Captain and his family suffered more than their fair share of grief before, during and after the war. His father died in early 1914. In February 1915 the second son, Captain/Commander Cecil Halstead France-Hayhurst died of pneumonia in Glasgow aged 40 years. He had recently taken command of *HMS Patricia* and left a wife and two daughters aged 6 and 8 years. Following closely on his death came news from France on 9 May 1915 that the eldest son, Colonel Frederick Charles France-Hayhurst, Royal Welsh Fusiliers, aged 45 years, had been killed in action. He had inherited the estate and title. The value of the estate at that time was put at £415,000. The brothers are commemorated on the Davenham Village war memorial. On a happier note, the remaining son, Captain W H France-Hayhurst, married his colonial bride Renee in York in June 1918. She was a South African and had lived in Cape Town. Their joy was short lived however, for Renee died in childbirth at York, just one year later.

Captain W H France-Hayhurst, and his bride Renee.

Not Forgotten

IN 1939, JUST 20 YEARS after the end of the Great War, humanity was once again threatened by Germany and her allies. This time it wasn't Kaiser Bill who had visions of Empire, but one Adolf Hitler and his Nazi Party who came to power in the mid-30s. In six short years this political grouping would plunge the world into the most dreadful conflict it had ever known. At the dawn of the new millennium, memories of the terror over which Hitler presided are still vivid in the minds of all those old enough to remember. Once again the men of Moulton responded to the call, and once again they marched down Main Road to fight for our liberty and freedom. 12 of their number marched into oblivion and their names are listed on the village War Memorial alongside the 34 who died in the Great War. They were:

> Brooks, Harold
> Buckley, Felix Frank
> Dickens, George
> Eyres, John Henry
> Goulding, Stanley
> Kendrick, James Eric
> Kennerley, Gordon
> Latham, Ralph
> Miles, George
> Shannon, George
> Stockall, Albert
> Wright, Frederick

God willing, these 12 men will be the subject of a separate study and dedication.

The Kaiser reviews his field artillery in preparation for war

1914

The Horror Begins

WHEN GAVRILO PRINCIP, a 19-year old Bosnian Serb militant, thrust his way forward in a Sarajevo street on 28 June 1914 he was only seconds away from collapsing a house of cards that would change the course of the 20th Century. The three shots he fired from the running board of the car carrying the Archduke Ferdinand and his wife, triggered a war that, even now evokes, not only sadness, but a feeling of utter hopelessness for those who died so tragically in the cause of liberty and freedom.

Princip's assassination of the Archduke Franz Ferdinand, heir to the thrones of Austria and Hungary, and his wife Sophie as they sat in their stationary open car, was a dreadful reminder of what one act of terrorism can achieve if performed at the right moment in time. The car, which had taken a wrong turning, was *en route* to the local hospital to allow the Archduke and his wife to visit a member of their staff, wounded earlier in the day, when a bomb had exploded nearby. Prophetically, it is believed that the registration plate on the car was 11.11.18. The ensuing conflict would eventually involve a total of 57 nations in the Great War of 1914 – 1918, now better known as World War One or the First World War.

Austro-Hungary charged Serbia with the assassinations. They demanding ten concessions, one requiring Serbia to put an immediate stop to the wave of anti-propaganda against Austro-Hungary sweeping Serbia at the time. Serbia, finding itself on a very sticky wicket, and having accepted advice from Great Britain and Russia, agreed to eight of the ten demands. This was not sufficient and on 28 July, Austro-Hungary declared war on Serbia. Russia, who had previously warned Austro-Hungary against such a move, began mobilisation. At this, Germany stepped in and threatened Russia that, if they did not stop mobilisation, they would have them to contend with. This was like a red rag to a bull, and Russia rejected

On the march though Belgium

the German threat out-of-hand. At this slap in the face, Germany declared war on Russia on 1 August. France then decided to climb aboard the wagon and began to mobilise. On 3 August, Germany decided to declare war on the French as well.

Great Britain who, until then, had tried to act as an honest broker, was drawn into the web. In early August the Belgians were informed by Germany of its intent to march through Belgium to stop the French from using the same route to attack them. In fact this move was part and parcel of the Schlieffen plan drawn up by Count Von Schliefffen between 1897 and 1905. The plan called for a massive blow in the French west, then to encircle Paris by way of Belgium. Naturally, Belgium refused to countenance this action and called on Great Britain to help. Great Britain who, as a signatory to an agreement dating back to 1839 guaranteeing Belgian neutrality, demanded that Germany withdraw their threat. This was refused, at which Great Britain declared war on Germany.

The die was cast.

On the 17 August, a British Expeditionary Force (BEF) commanded by Field Marshal Sir John French, comprising regular and territorial units, was despatched post haste to France. Liege had fallen the day before and the German armies were well on their way, marching through Belgium. On 23/24 August, the British force came to grips with a vastly superior German one at the Belgium town of Mons. With the French retreating on both their right and left, and in danger of being out-flanked, the BEF itself began to retreat. It should be emphasised that this was no rout, for the retreat was conducted strategically, and in good order. The discipline shown by the BEF was superb as it fought, retreated, turned about and fought again, all the way back to the River Marne. The old adage that 'He who fights and runs away, lives to fight another day' was never so true as with the retreat of the BEF from Mons to the River Marne. On 3 September, having retreated 200 miles, it crossed the River Marne and dug-in. After re-grouping, pontoon bridges were built across the river and, on 9 September, the BEF advanced into a gap that had opened on the German right. The enemy, under the command of General Von Bulow, panicked, and immediately began to withdraw. The battle of the Marne was as good as won, with the Gemans withdrawing to positions along the River Aisne. Then came the 'race to the sea' to safeguard (or to occupy in the German case) the Channel ports.

On 9 October, Antwerp fell to the Germans and the Belgian garrison together with the British Naval Brigade escaped westwards towards the Dutch border. The British 7th Division and 3rd Cavalry Division, which had landed at Zeebrugge and Ostende on the 6th, 7th and 8th October, helped cover the Belgian retreat through West Flanders and arrived at Ypres on the 14th. The British II and III Corps from the Aisne reached a line behind Hazebrouck and La Bassée on the 10–11 October. The I Corps entered Ypres on the 20th. The Allies fought off German attacks in the Battle of the Yser (18 October to 30 November) and the First Battle of Ypres (30 October to 24 November) in which the BEF were virtually eliminated while stopping the German forward movement. Huge losses of life were inflicted on both the British and German sides, with German losses so severe that General Eric Von Falkenhayn acknowledged that casualties of this magnitude could not be sustained, and wound down his onslaught on the what was to become known as the Ypres Salient. The name Ypres would become a household name in Britain as the war progressed, as was the name of the Somme after July 1916.

Today, over 80 years on, at 8 o'clock every evening, buglers of the Ypres Fire Brigade sound *Last Post* and *Reveille* under the arches of the Menin Gate memorial. This poignant sounding has taken place every evening since the unveiling of the monument in 1929, except during the German occupation of the town in the Second World War, although the sounding recommenced the very day the occupying force was driven from the town. The Menin Gate Memorial was constructed after the war to honour the 54,361 missing of the British Empire who fell in the Ypres Salient between October 1914 and 15-16 August 1917.

By December, deadlock had set-in on the Western Front. The attempt by Austria to take Serbia failed miserably and they scuttled back over their borders in December, having lost over 20,000 officers and men. A line of Allied and German trenches and dugouts faced each other from the Belgium coast to the Swiss border, a distance of nearly 500 miles. The war of movement had ceased. It is probably true to state that, for the remainder of the war, the Germans looked down on the allied from superior positions.

As 1914 ended, the BEF was bleeding badly and in need of a life-saving transfusion. This was at hand, for Lord Kitchener's call for volunteers had resulted in over a million men enlisting in the New Armies in the first few months of the conflict. The 'Service' or 'K' battalions as they were known were preparing to enter the fray.

Other Fronts

By the end of 1914 fighting had broken out in other theatres apart from the Western Fronts of France and Belgium. In Africa, German forces surrendered in Togoland and Cameroon. On the Russian front the battles of Tannenberg and the Masurian Lakes ended inconclusively with the Russians slipping away to fight another day.

On the Oceans of the world the British and German fleets tested each others mettle. Ships on both sides joined Davy Jones in the battles of the Heligoland Bight, Coronel and the Falkland Islands. The east coast towns of Hartlepool, Whitby and Scarborough were shelled by German battleships standing offshore. On 9 November the German raider *Emden* was sunk by *HMS Sydney* after having created havoc for some months to the ships of the Mercantile Marine.

Moulton

Young and not so young men from Moulton took the King's shilling, and by the end of the war 230 of them had enrolled out of a total village population of 1,100. A magnificent response, and one of which Moulton should be very proud.

There may be only 'One way in and one way out of the village' but the men of 1914–1918 knew where their duty lay and marched down Main Road to the recruiting offices and, sadly, in some cases into oblivion. They served, and some died, in distant corners of Europe, Africa, Palestine, India and on the high seas.

Over 70 men in the last quarter of the year had marched off to join their regiments, amongst them a large proportion of married men.

By the end of 1914 the people of Moulton had adjusted their lives to the war and to their new circumstances but, during October, the real tragedy of war left its mark on the village. **John Crank**, was dead, albeit from natural causes brought on by a horrendous channel crossing on his way to France, and another, Charles Hampton had been wounded. The future looked bleak.

Dedicated to the Memory of John Crank

John Crank holds the unenviable record of being the first soldier from the village to die in the Great War. He was born at Kelsall on 17 December 1881. His parents, James and Mary, like so many families in those days, moved house frequently. In 1881 they were to be found living, with their four children, James 15, Mary 10, Frances 8, and Peter (Alex?), a 4-year old, in Yeld Lane in the Eddisbury Census district. By the mid 1880s they had moved to Chapel Lane, Moulton and, in 1891, were settled at 67 Main Road with their children James now 25, Frances 18, Peter (Alex?) 14 and John, their 'latest arrival', now 9-years old. At the time of his death in 1914, John and his widowed mother Mary, were living at 8 Chapel Lane, Moulton. John was his mother's sole means of support.

John Crank enlisted in Northwich at the very start of the war and was immediately drafted into the Royal Army Service Corps as a transport driver. By September 1914 he was stationed in Antwerp, Belgium and it was here, in late October, that his health broke down. Just before the Germans occupied Antwerp on 10th October, John was hospitalised to Fort Pitt Hospital, Chatham where his condition deteriorated. He died at home on 30 October aged 32 years. His funeral took place on 4 November and he was interred at St. Wilfrid's Churchyard, Davenham in the afternoon. Many villagers watched and grieved as the cortège, the coffin draped with a Union Jack, passed slowly down Main Road and out of the village.

In July 1915 John Crank was commemorated on the Moulton Roll of Honour in the Parish magazine. On 21 November 1915, a Memorial Service was held in St. Stephen's Parish Church for John and three other Moultoners; William Jervis Clarke. George Weedon, and George Greatbanks, who had by this time paid the supreme sacrifice.

Private John Crank

John Crank, Private No. M2/11447
Royal Army Service Corps
Died at home on Friday, 30 October 1914. Age 32
He is buried in St. Wilfred Churchyard, Davenham, Cheshire

Private John Crank's headstone in St.Wilfrid Churchyard

Private John Crank

John Crank's Awards

The 1914 Star   The British War Medal   The Victory Medal

John Crank is also commemorated on the
Moulton Methodist Church Tablet

The memorial tablet in Moulton Methodist Church.

Private John Crank

In 1891 John was living
at 67 Main Road, with
his mother father and
four brothers and sisters

8 Chapel Lane, the house
in which John Crank died
in October 1914

Artillery has no respect for night or day

1915

STALEMATE

1915 SAW THE CONSOLIDATION of the trench systems along the whole of the Western Front. In places, the German and Allied trenches were as little as 30-yards apart and men could be heard talking, singing and generally going about their everyday chores by the enemy opposite. Trenches were deepened, duckboards laid, fire-steps and dugouts improved and barbed wire to the front of each trench thickened. To minimise casualties from blast, the trenches were dug in a zig-zag fashion and support, reserve and communication trenches were worked on. Men could spend up to six days standing in these open ditches, in all weathers and conditions. They would creep forward, usually at night, along the communication trench to relieve the battalion in residence. Having done their stint, the relieved men would retire to the rear for four days to wash, eat proper meals, clean their gear and sleep off their exhaustion in shelters and in reasonable comfort. Their mud-encrusted uniforms were washed and fumigated, for lice plagued the men to distraction. Lice managed to get everywhere and the men spent hours running lighted matches, candles or even cigarettes along the seams of their clothes to incinerate the little devils who seemed hell bent on making their uncomfortable lives even more difficult. Having rested and generally restored themselves to sanity, the troops would then move into reserve for a further four days, before performing another stint in the front line trenches. And so the cycle continued: four days in the line, four days rest and then four days in reserve.

Lord Kitchener's New Army volunteers, very often serving in the City or 'Pals' Battalions, as some became affectionately known, were completing their training and joining their divisions abroad. The idea of Pals battalions, keeping together men from the same district, was sound in principle. They very often knew each other, spoke with the same dialect and had a fierce pride in their battalions. Examples of these battalions were the Accrington Pals, Liverpool and Manchester Pals, Grimsby Chums and University Regiments. The Glasgow Boy's Brigade formed a battalion of Boy's Brigade old boys from the city. Later in the war, this battalion lost 514 of its 1,000 strength on 1 July 1916, the opening of the Battle of the Somme. The Accrington Pals lost 585 the same day and, worst of all, the 10th West Yorks. (Leeds and Harrogate) lost 710 officers and men. For, what could not be foreseen, was that many of these battalions would be wiped out in a matter of hours and that 'angels of death', in the guise of postmen and telegraph boys, would deliver their messages of doom and anguish by the bagfull to small communities up and down the country.

Major battles occurred at Neuve-Chapelle and St. Eloi in March and April. On 22 April the Second Battle of Ypres opened. The Ypres Salient, extending ten miles across its base and five miles deep, was faced on three sides by eleven German Divisions. Just before 5.00 pm on the 22nd, the German guns, which had been pounding the Salient all day, fell silent. The spring sun was about to drop below the horizon when the town and surrounding villages were subjected to another fearful bombardment. Squinting over their front line trenches to see if the bombardment was to be the prelude to a frontal attack, the troops saw a greenish-yellow fog

Gas mask parade

creeping towards them. Chlorine gas was about to join the weapons of war *Dulce et decorum est Pro patria mori*' ("It is sweet and fitting to die for one's Country" – the last lines of Wilfred Owen's poem about men dying in a gas attack). As the gas enveloped the French and Algerian troops, they fled, allowing the Germans following behind their gas cloud, to claim a huge piece of the Salient.

All along the front from April to September, battles raged at St. Julian, Aubers Ridge, Festubert, and Vimy Ridge, culminating in the Battle of Loos at the end of September. At Loos the British, who by now had added gas to their own weaponry, released chlorine gas prior to their attack. In some sectors this was successful in driving the enemy out of their front line trenches. In other parts of the line the wind suddenly changed direction, with the result that the gas either hung about in No-Man's Land like a great festering cloud, or worse, blew back into the faces of the men about to go forward.

Despite initial gains the French were unsuccessful in their attempt to take Vimy Ridge, neither were the Guards successful in their efforts to capture the notorious Hill 70 east of Loos. German counter-attacks later negated most of the gains made at the start of the battle.

Men of the R.H.A. in trenches at Aubers Ridge

New Zealand infantry dug-in on the ridges above Anzac Cove, Gallipoli

Other fronts

In the early part of 1915, a decision was taken to open up another front at Gallipoli to allow the British fleet unimpeded access through the Dardanelles and into the Sea of Marmara and the Black Sea beyond. After an initial bombardment in mid-February, coupled with a small landing on the Gallipoli peninsula, an attempt was made to sail through the narrows into the inland sea. The Turkish forces, having been given four weeks to ready themselves, destroyed three Allied battleships and badly disabled three others with both mines and gunfire from the heights above the narrows. The operation was then called-off and never again attempted.

At dawn on 25 April the Expeditionary Force gathered in Murdos Bay and landed at three points along the coast. The force comprised Australian, British, French and New Zealand troops. By nightfall a toe-hold had been achieved at all landing points, but losses were heavy. The Turks, under German command, were well dug-in on the heights – waiting as the attacking force came ashore.

For the next eight months the Allies continued to sustain terrible losses in their attempt to subjugate the Turks. All their efforts came to nought and places such as Sulva Bay, Anzac Cove and Cape Helles would go down in folklore as killing grounds where men gave their all to no avail. On the night of 9 January 1916, having decided that their losses were too heavy to bear, the last of the Allied troops crept quietly down to the beaches, climbed aboard their landing craft and sailed off into the blackness. Next day the Turks and Germans awakened to find empty trenches in all sectors of the Allied line – the birds had flown.

Between May and December, the Central Powers waged a fearsome assault on the Russian Army in an attempt to drive them back from the Carpathian Mountains and thereby rid Austria of the 'Bear' on their doorstep. Over 600,000 German troops took part against an enemy three times as large. By early October the Russians had been driven back to a line in front of Minsk and although not beaten, were so badly weakened that they were never a serious threat again.

On the Italian fronts battles for Isonzo raged from June until November. In Palestine the Turks attacked the Suez Canal and, in July, the last of the German forces surrendered in South Africa .

At sea the battle of Dogger Bank took place in January. The liners *Lusitania* and *Arabic* were sent to the bottom along with the German *Dresden* and the French *Leon Gambetta*.

Men of the Cheshire Regiment at training camp somewher in England

1915 – STALEMATE

Moulton

By the end of January 100 men from the village had enlisted, including 17 Army Reservists. Their names were published in the Northwich Guardian and included 17 of those who subsequently died. In March a dance was organised raising £1 for the Belgium Relief Fund. Because of the war, a decision was taken in May to cancel the village festival.

In the same month the Council School published a Roll of Honour listing the names of 78 former pupils who had joined the armed forces. In July the Parish Magazine followed suit with a full list of all those serving. These two publications had a double-edged effect on the men of the village. Firstly, they cemented the bond of comradeship between those who had enlisted and secondly, acted as a spur to those of eligible age in the village who had not at that time stepped forward.

Mr J Winstanly, landlord of the Red Lion, with his 'Soldiers Christmas Cheer Fund', was determined that every man from the village should receive a quality Christmas gift. Various functions were organised including a dance in The Verdin Institute, with singing by local vocalists. Refreshments were provided and a total of £3.5s.0p. was raised. On another occasion The institute band, joined by members of the Over Silver Band, paraded through the village collecting 30s, *en route*.

A football match – Moulton Alexandra v Over Congos swelled the coffers of the Christmas Cheer Fund to £32. This was increased by one guinea (£1.1s.0p) when the manager of the local Picture Palace decided to contribute a percentage of his takings to the fund. Others in the village were also raising of funds for parcels. The Verdin Institute organised a Potato Pie Supper in December and Mr and Mrs Rains of the Travellers Rest raised sufficient money to send every soldier a Christmas parcel containing cigarettes and other goodies. After Christmas many letters of gratitude were received from the troops for these parcels which had helped brighten their terrible conditions. One letter, from Sergeant J Burnes, said that they were billeted in an old barn some three miles from the firing line, and that wrapping paper, cards and photographs were used to decorate the barn walls for Christmas. On 21 November a memorial service was held in the Parish Church for those who had died. They were **John Crank, William Clarke, George Weedon** and **George Greatbanks**. Another of the Moulton fallen, **Wilmot Buckley,** was killed in action at the Battle of Loos on 3 October, but presumabley his death had not been confirmed at the time of the memorial service.

Dedicated to the Memory of Wilmot Buckley

Wilmot Buckley was born in Moulton on 24 July 1885. He attended the village Council school and is shown on its May 1915 Roll of Honour as serving with the 3rd Battalion, the Cheshire Regiment. His parents, Mark and Lucy Buckley, appear to have had gypsy blood in their veins, for they moved house regularly. In 1881 they lived with their six children and one other (Sarah Preston – aged 8) at 17 Moulton Lane (Main Road), in 1885 at 53 Main Road and, in 1891, they had moved to 24 Main Road. By this time the family had increased by three, although this was negated by the fact that three of the originals were no longer at home, possibly married or working away. Mark earned his living as a Salt Boiler, very likely at the Newbridge Salt Works, close by the village.

At the outbreak of war Wilmot was in lodgings with his married sister, Mrs Galley, at 49 Main Road and, at sometime in mid-1915 along with many of his pals from the village, was posted to the Western Front with the 2nd Battalion, the Cheshire Regiment. On 7 October his sister, Mrs Galley, received a letter from him to say that he was well.

The Battle of Loos was fought from 24 September to 4 November. On 3 October, 30-year old Wilmot Buckley was killed. By all accounts he went over the top in company with some of his village friend and, after the action, Wilmot and his chum George Greatbanks, did not answer roll call. It would seem they had died together, somewhere in No-Man's Land.

The Regimental History account of the action reads:

… On 3rd October, the Germans attacked all along the line of 84th Brigade, but were repulsed except on the left where they gained a footing… A bayonet counter attack, led by Major Roddy, was met with a hail of bombs and driven back to the British front line,

Wilmot's body was never recovered and his name is commemorated on the Loos Memorial to the Missing at Pas de Calais. He is in good company – John Kipling, son of the poet, Rudyard and Fergus Bowes-Lyon, brother of the Queen Mother are also commemorated on the memorial.

Private Wilmot Buckley

Wilmot Buckley, Private No. 25893
2nd Battalion, The Cheshire Regiment
Killed in Action, Sunday 3 October 1915. Age 30
His name is commemorated on
The Loos Memorial to the Missing, Pas de Calais, France. Panels 49 – 50

The Loos Memorial in Dud Corner Cemetery, Pas de Calais, France

Private Wilmot Buckley

Wilmot Buckley's Awards

The 1914–1915 Star   The British War Medal   The Victory Medal

Private Wilmot Buckley is also commemorated on the
Moulton Methodist Church Tablet

In Sacred Memory
of
those connected
with this church and school,
who made the supreme sacrifice in the Great War
1914 – 1919.

ASHLEY SAM	FOSTER JACK	RAVENSCROFT GEO.
BUCKLEY ROBERT	GROVES HARRY	SHAW JOSEPH
BUCKLEY ROBERT H.	HITCHINSON HORACE	SOUTHERN JAMES
BUCKLEY WILMOT	HODKINSON HARRY	SOUTHERN THOMAS
CLARKE JERVIS	LUNT WILLIE	TOMLINSON DAN.
CLARKE WILLIAM J.	LUNT GEORGE	TOMLINSON ENOCH
COOKSON WILLIAM H.	MADDOCK JACK	TOMLINSON JOHN
CRANK JOHN	NODEN ARTHUR	WAKEFIELD PETER
DIDSBURY WALTER	PRICE ELIJAH	WEEDON GEORGE

The memorial tablet in Moulton Methodist Church.

Dedicated to the Memory of William Jervis Clarke

At the beginning of January 1915 the weather in the English Channel was at its most malevolent. The seas were ferocious as the troop ship carrying young William Jervis Clarke clawed it's way towards France. William was violently ill and on arrival was promptly bundled off to the nearest hospital. Some days later he developed 'Brain Fever' (Meningitis?) and died from this condition on Tuesday 26 January. He was 20-years old.

It is worth recording that on William's Medal Roll card, held in the Public Records Office at Kew, a scribbled note states "Died of D" – could this have been Dysentery?

William was born in Moulton at Bank Farm on 7 October 1894. He was the son of Jessie and Betsy(?) Clarke and, on leaving Moulton Council school, secured employment as an apprentice motor engineer with Mr J N Stubbs of the Arcade, Winsford, were he was very popular.

At the outbreak of war he is recorded as living at 82 Regent Street, Moulton and it was from here that he went to Chester to enlist in the Royal Garrison Artillery as a mechanic. Later he was transferred to the Royal Army Service Corps. In 1915 his name is shown on both the Parish and School Rolls of Honour as having paid the supreme sacrifice.

On 14 February 1915 a memorial service was held for William at the Primitive Methodist Church. In December 1915 St Stephen's Church held a joint Memorial Service for him and three other village soldiers, John Crank, George Weedon and George Greatbanks. A large congregation attended both services, including relatives, friends and work mates.

Private William Jervis Clarke

William Jervis Clarke, Private No. M2/021253
169th Company, Royal Army Service Corps
Died on Tuesday, 26 January 1915. Age 20
Buried at St. Sever Cemetery, Rouen, France. A II. 22

William Jervis Clarke's headstone at St. Sever Cemetery

Private William Jervis Clarke

William Jervis Clarke's Awards

The British War Medal   The Victory Medal

Private William Jervis Clarke is also commemorated on the
Moulton Methodist Church Tablet

In Sacred Memory
of
those connected
with this church and school,
who made the supreme sacrifice in the Great War
1914 – 1919.

Ashley Sam	Foster Jack	Ravenscroft Geo.
Buckley Robert	Croves Harry	Shaw Joseph
Buckley Robert H.	Hitchinson Horace	Southern James
Buckley Wilmot	Hodkinson Harry	Southern Thomas
Clarke Jervis	Lunt Willie	Tomlinson Dan.
Clarke William J.	Lunt George	Tomlinson Enoch
Cookson William H.	Maddock Jack	Tomlinson John
Crank John	Noden Arthur	Wakefield Peter
Didsbury Walter	Price Elijah	Weedon George

The memorial tablet in Moulton Methodist Church.

Dedicated to the Memory of George Greatbanks

George Greatbanks was a Winsford man who moved to 5 Chapel Lane, Moulton after his marriage to Clara Annie. Prior to the War he was employed as a chemical worker at Brunner Mond's Winnington site.

At the very outset of the war, George enlisted in Northwich but was discharged as unfit – he was missing a finger from his right hand. He was recalled to the colours on 14 April 1915 and sailed for France with the 2nd Battalion, the Cheshire Regiment on 23 June. In July George is shown on the Parish Roll of Honour. Three of his brothers also served in the Army and one, J W Greatbanks, was captured at the Battle of Mons.

Annie received two letters a week from George, who regularly described the conditions he was experiencing. In August he wrote of the narrow escape he had whilst firing from between some sandbags. He had "helped a German down with – a bit of bad" as he put it. As he ducked down into the trench a bullet hit the sandbag where his head had been seconds before. He kept the bullet as a souvenir,

The Battle of Loos was fought between 24 September to 4 November 1915 and, on 3 October, during the battle, George Greatbanks was killed – he was 27-years old. By all accounts he went over the top in company with many of his friends from the village. After the engagement, George and his chum, Wilmot Buckley, did not answer their names at roll call. It would seem that they had died together, somewhere in the devastation of No-Mans Land.

The account in the Regimental History reads:

.... On 3rd October, the Germans attacked all along the line of 84th Brigade, but were repulsed except on the left where they gained a footing.... A bayonet counter-attack, led by Major Roddy, was met with a hail of bombs and driven back to the British line.*

The news that George was missing was first received in a letter from an old Northwich Vics footballer, Harry (Kelly) Birkenhead, to his wife living in Main Road. She immediately passed the news on to Annie Greatbanks.

In early November, and sometime after Annie had been advised officially of her husbands 'missing' status, she received a letter from Company Sergeant Major McIntyre, 1st Battalion, Scots Guards in which he said that one of his patrols had come across the body of a soldier in No-Man's Land. Before they buried the body they searched his pockets and retrieved a letter from which Sergeant Major obtained her address. The letter was enclosed – it was one Annie had written to George earlier.

The grave of George Greatbanks was later lost in the heat of battle. His name can now be found on the Loos Memorial to the Missing at Pas de Calais along with his pal, Wilmot Buckley. They are in good company, for the names of John Kipling, son of the poet, Rudyard and Fergus Bowes-Lyon, brother of the Queen Mother are also inscribed there.

Sometime after the war Annie re-married and became Mrs Clara Annie Dahin and settled in Hainaut, Belgium. Maybe she met her new husband whilst on a visit to the memorial at Loos. Who knows?

On 21 November 1915 a memorial service was held in St. Stephen's Church for George Greatbanks, John Crank, William Clarke and George Weedon. Strange that Wilmot Buckley's name was not included in the service. Maybe he was still in the 'missing' category.

These last two paragraphs are more or less a mirror of the report in Wilmot Buckley's dedication.

Private William George Greatbanks

George Greatbanks, Private No. 25924
2nd Battalion, The Cheshire Regiment
Killed in Action, Sunday 3 October 1915. Age 27
His name is commemorated on
The Loos Memorial to the Missing, Pas de Calais, France. Panels 49 – 50

The Loos Memorial in Dud Corner Cemetery, Pas de Calais, France

Private William George Greatbanks

George Greatbanks' Awards

The 1914 –1915 Star   The British War Medal   The Victory Medal

---

Other Memorial commemorating George Greatbanks' name

Brunner Mond War Memorial, Winnington.

Winsford Town War Memorial

5 Chapel Street, Moulton, where George Greenbanks lived

Dedicated to the Memory of George Weedon

George Weedon was born in Jack Lane, Moulton in 1882. His parents, Charles and Ellen Weedon were 32 and 25 respectively at the time of his birth. His two older siblings were Ester and William. Charles was a Salt Boiler, most probably at Newbridge Salt Works on the banks of the Weaver Navigation. Sometime before George's 9th birthday the family moved from Jack Lane to 34 Regents Street and, along with other village children, attended the local council school.

Some years before the outbreak of war, George moved from the salt village to work in Stafford. He married a local girl there and they had a child, a boy, also named George.

George served for a number of years with the Royal Welch Fusiliers before being discharged into the reserve. He re-joined the regulars at Northwich in August 1914 and was posted to the 2nd Battalion of his old regiment. The Battalion's War Diary for 16 May 1915 reads:

Bombardment of enemy's wire opposite Middlesex Regiment (on the left flank of the RWF) at 11.15 am and 6.0 pm. Very quiet on our front – one man killed

That man was Lance-Corporal George Weedon. A letter from a friend stated that George was cooking breakfast at the back of a trench near Bois Grenier, some two miles from Armentières, when he was sniped in the head. On the way to the field hospital George succumbed to his wound. He was 33-years old.

He is mentioned in the July 1915 Parish Roll of Honour. At that time he was one of three men from Moulton who had made the supreme sacrifice. On Sunday, 21 November 1915 a memorial service was held in St. Stephen's Parish Church for George and three other soldiers who had died. They were John Crank, William J Clarke and George Greatbanks.

Some time after his death George's wife re-married and their son (George junior) came to live at Lodge Farm, Moulton with his Aunt Ester. Nora Hickson, Esters daughter, now living in Lawrence Avenue, remembers the little boy as being rather frail.

George's father Charles died during the war and his mother Ellen moved to 17 Church Street. Their eldest son William, serving in the 10th Royal Hussars, survived the conflict.

Lance-Corporal George Weedon

George Weedon, Lance-Corporal No. 8165
2nd Battalion, The Royal Welch Fusiliers
Killed in Action, Sunday 16 May 1915. Age 33
He is buried in Bois Grenier Cemetery, France. D I

George Weedon's headstone in Bois Grenier Cemetery

Lance-Corporal George Weedon

George Weedon's Awards

| The 1914 Star | The British War Medal | The Victory Medal |

Lance-Corporal George Weedon is also commemorated on the
Moulton Methodist Church Tablet

The memorial tablet in Moulton Methodist Church.

An ambulance passing through one of the Western Front's many war-torn villages

1916

DEATH ON A SUMMER'S DAY

U NTIL THE BEGINNING OF 1916, every man in the British Army was either a professional, territorial or volunteer soldier. This was to change in February when conscription was introduced for all men fit for service between the ages of 18 and 41 years of age, unmarried, or childless widower. In May married men were also included.

On 30 May, the British Grand Fleet commanded by Admiral Sir John Jellicoe sailed on patrol in the North Sea with the expectation of meeting up with the German High Seas Fleet commanded by Admiral Reinhard Scheer – he was not disappointed. On 31 May the fleets met at Jutland off the Danish coast where a tremendous battle took place. On 1 June, when the German fleet turned for home, over 6,000 British and 2,500 German sailors had perished. The British had lost 14 capital ships against Germany's 11. Although heavier armour-plating on the German ships saved many from going to the bottom, many of them were so badly damaged that a number were not fully operational again for months. On the other hand, the British Fleet remained in control of the seas off Scandinavia – a marginal victory for Jellicoe, but only just.

Ironically, mines laid by the Germans just prior to the battle were to inflict a far greater blow than German High Command could ever have envisaged. On 5 June the British Secretary of State for War, Field Marshal Lord Kitchener, travelling aboard *HMS Hampshire* on his way to Russia heading a military mission, was killed when the *Hampshire* was sunk off Marwick Head, Orkney when it hit one of these mines .

From February to December 1916, in an attempt to break the spirit of French resistance and resolve, the German Army prepared to sacrifice itself on the fortress altar of Verdun. The French were determined that they would not succeed – 'We stand here' they said. 'Ils ne passeront pas' (They shall not pass). The 'Mincing machine of Verdun', as the battle became known, centred around the defences in the heights close to the city. Rings of forts, of which Fort Douaumont on the right bank of the River Meuse was the most dominant at over 1,000 feet, stood between the Germans and their objective. The fighting raged back and forth for most of the year with neither side gaining an advantage. As the year neared its close, the combatants counted their losses: France 400,000; Germany 350,000. Neither side fully recovered from the slaughter at Verdun, and for this reason, it became one of the defining battles of the war.

Talk of a 'Big Push' was much in evidence in the spring of 1916. French Allied Commander, General Joffre, planned an assault in the area of the River Somme. Two French and one British Army Corps were to break through enemy lines on a 60 mile front but, because of the decimation of the French Army at Verdun, its contribution was reduced – the British, commanded by Field Marshal Sir Douglas Haig, were obliged to take on the lions' share of the attack. Haig was against the Somme offensive. He felt there was a much better chance of success in Flanders. However, he was overruled by Joffre who was hell-bent on a war of attrition.

For seven days and nights prior to the battle, Allied artillery pounded the enemy lines without respite. Far behind the German front, rail-yards, camps and headquarters were hit and, on the night of 25 June the town of Combles and it's railhead was struck by 3,000 heavy shells with the

LA BORNE.   THUS FAR AND NO FURTHER.

A postcard, produced by the French for the English market, high-lighting their efforts at Verdun

result that an ammunition train was blown sky-high in the station. Every man, from ranking officer to lowly 'Tommy', believed that nothing could survive the onslaught – the German trenches, along with their masses of protective barbed-wire, would be totally destroyed, leaving the British infantry free to walk across No-Mans Land to occupy the enemy lines and sort out the devastation. How wrong they were. For 18 months the industrious Germans had been digging into the chalk hills above the Allied line, resulting in a strong system of three trench lines, each protected by thick belts of wire entaglements. They had excavated spacious dug-outs deep into the chalk for protection against shelling. On the spurs of the hillsides, concrete and sandbagged fortresses had been built to provide enfilade fields of fire for their Maxim machine guns.

On 1 June, the British Minister of Labour, Mr Arthur Henderson, talking to a group of managers and munition workers in Leeds, let the cat out of the bag when he said:

> I am asked why the Whitsuntide holidays are to be postponed until the end of July. How inquisitive we all are! It should suffice that we ask for a postponement of the holidays until the end of July. This fact should speak volumes.

It did indeed. His remarks were reported in the National Press and the Germans were aware within hours of both the 'when' and the 'where' and, in the early hours of 1 July, a German listening post at La Boisselle picked up General Rawlinson's 'Good luck' wish to the British 4th Army.

At 7.20 am on the 1 July (General Rawlinson wanted to attack before dawn, but again, the French overruled the British) 100,000 men, mostly made up of Kitchener's New Army volunteers, massed in their front line trenches. Suddenly the 1,500 guns, which had been firing without a break for over a week, fell silent. The air became still as the early morning sun warmed the backs of the troops below. Choirs of larks sang their morning chorus as the men waited for the whistles to signal that the time had come for them to go 'over the top'. At Hawthorne Redoubt and La Boisselle, two huge ammonal mines laid under the German front line trenches by Royal Engineers' Tunnelling Companies blew, the one under Hawthorne Redoubt leaving a crater 35-yards wide by 20-yards deep.

At 7.30 am, along 18 miles of the British front, the whistles sounded and the men climbed onto their scaling ladders and out of their trenches. They were fully loaded with packs, entrenching tools, rifles, ammunition, bombs and barbed-wire, ready to take-over and consolidate the German front line. These they believed, had been totally destroyed. Colonels and

Going 'over the top'

A German machine gun nest on the Somme

other senior officers walked in front of their men, some sporting walking sticks. The enemy, although having taken heavy losses in the bombardment, were still a disciplined fighting force. The survivors emerged from their bunkers, 20–30 feet deep below the chalky ground, mounted their machine guns and mowed-down lines of the advancing infantry. On nearing the German trenches, officers and men saw to their horror that, in most places, the wire was uncut. Shells, meant to have destroyed dug-outs and wire alike, had failed to do their work. Countless numbers of them were defective, laying there on the ground were they had fallen. Others were just not up to the task of penetrating the deep German shelters. The effect of swathes of uncut wire meant that men headed for the few gaps which had been created, making the job of the German machine gunners even easier. Mounds of bodies soon began to fill the gaps in the wire. The net result of all this carnage was that few objectives were achieved, and most of those that where, had to be forfeited when the efforts of flanking units failed.

At the day's end, and for very little gain, the British took nearly 60,000 casualties of whom 20,000 were killed. Among those lying dead or dying in the July sunshine was Corporal Joseph Yardley of Moulton Village.

The Battle of the Somme came to a halt in the November of 1916. Today it overshadows all other actions of the Great War. It cost Great Britain and the Commonwealth over 400,000 casualties, the French 200,000 and estimates of German dead and wounded vary from between 500,000 and 700,000.

Attrition had come of age.

In the summer of 1916, bulky, tarpaulin-covered machines were shipped to France under close guard. Early drawings had described them as 'Water Transporters for Mesopotamia' but during their trip to France those guarding them, when asked, described them as "mobile tanks for fuel and water storage". On 15 September at Flers, a number of these 'fuel and water storage tanks' were used in action for the first time and, apart from the fuel they carried, and no doubt some water, they proved to be much more than mere 'storage taks'. The 'Tank', a named still used today, was born. In their first action, some suffered mechanical problems before reaching their jumping-off points, others ditched, but the 11 which crossed the German line put the fear of God into the German troops. One straddled the line, using machine guns to clear the trench, and 300 enemy troops surrendered. A Tank Memorial now marks the spot on the Bapaume–Albert road from which these first 'tanks' went into action .

Other Fronts

In the Caucasus, the Russians and Turks were engaged in heavy fighting resulting in major gains for the Russians when the Turks turned and fled. Alarmed, Turkish High Command sent their Second Army to the rescue. This move stabilised the situation and, by August, the Russians were on their knees, unwilling to go further.

In Italy, the fighting in the Isonzo continued throughout the year. In November the 9th battle took place with more to come. May and June saw Field Marshal Conrad and his Austrians attack on a 20-mile front at Trentino in the Austrian Tyrol. It came as no surprise to the Italians who, after backing off for five miles, held the Austrians until they wilted. Conrad then decided to scale down this operation and to concentrate his efforts on breaking through on the Isonzo front instead.

In Mesopotamia a combined British and Indian force, under siege for five months by a superior Turkish Force, was finally compelled to surrender with the loss of over 10,000 troops. In December, Bucharest fell to a combined Austrian–German onslaught.

Moulton

In February James Needham, landlord of the Red Lion at Winsford, was prosecuted for falling foul of a new military law. His offence – allowing a soldier on home leave to have a pint after 9 pm.

The first official photograph of a tank going into action

On 2 June, the Winsford Guardian records the names of Moulton men serving with the Cheshire Regiment and wounded during recent fighting The article went on to say. that Corporal A Whitlow of the Royal Army Medical Corps had treated a number of lads including Bob Buckley. Walter Didsbury of 9 Regent Street had been wounded in his right shoulder and was in Cheltenham Hospital, where he was expected to make a good recovery.

In a letter from the front to his mother in Chapel Street, Private Harry Noden said he had met up with his two brothers, George and Arthur, for the first time in 18 months. Two Winsford lads, also named Noden, were there too, and they all enjoyed a good night out together.

In September, Mr H W Bowker, the Council School headmaster, received letters and cards from old scholars on the school Roll of Honour. They showed how touched the men were to have been remembered and to have received parcels. Corporal Archie Whitlow, summed up the feelings saying he wished to thank the teachers and scholars alike for their kindness to him. "I have pleasant memories of my school days", he concluded. In a another, sent in November, Archie said that:

> ... had seen a cavalry charge a few days ago ... it was a fine sight. It was great to see the enemy with their hands up. I was bowled over by a shell, but I escaped injury but had quite a fright. I met two of the lads (G. Didsbury and W. Hodkinson) a few days ago. The weather is wretched, rain day after day and mud everywhere. You will be pleased to hear that I won a Brigade race about a month ago. I captained our team and we won all the way.

Under the heading 'Patriotic Villagers' the Winsford Guardian reported in December that in the early days of the war Moulton's response for men had been magnificent. The villagers were now very keen to ensure that all of their 170 soldier boys were kept supplied with all kinds of comforts. Parcels are sent regularly from a committee Chaired by Mr J J Tomlinson with Secretaries Messrs J Winstanly and W Taylor. A fund opened a little while ago to send a Christmas gift to each Moulton man was so successful that a postal order for 6s. 6d was also sent along with a customised Christmas card and letter from the villagers.

Nevertheless, 1916 was a sad year for Moulton. In May, **Sam Ashley** was thought to have been killed (It was later confirmed that he had been taken prisoner). Sadly, he died while in enemy hands with no reason given for his death. On 1 July **Joseph Yardley** was klled in the Battle of the Somme, and **Robert H Buckley, Robert Buckley, Jervis Clarke** and **Joseph Shaw** were to fall before the month drew to a close.

Dedicated to the Memory of Sam Ashley

In the Moulton Council School's record of 1910, Sam Ashley was voted 'Most Popular Boy', by his school pals. Sam lost none of this good nature or popularity as he matured into manhood. In June 1915 his platoon sergeant, Sergeant Byrne wrote to Sam's father offering him his condolences, when it was thought that Sam had perished. He went on to say that 'Sam had a very cheery disposition, with a pleasant smile and was very well liked and respected by both men and officers alike'.

Sam was born on 5 September 1896 and lived with his parents at 27 Regent Street until called-up for service. He attended the village council school and took part in many after-school activities, including membership of the Black Minstrel Troop. After leaving school he worked in the District County Surveyors Office in Northwich. He enlisted in autumn 1914 and was included in both the school and village Rolls of Honour of 1915. His two brothers also served in the Army. Sam was posted to the 10th Battalion, The Cheshire Regiment.

In early November 1915, after completing his training, Sam found himself crossing the Channel *en route* for France. The Battalion arrived at dawn and proceeded up-country to the firing line. They remained in the trenches for four days, witnessing at first hand a bombardment just along the line from where they were positioned. This was followed by a battle which Sam was not permitted to name. However, it seems it was the battle of Nonne Boschen. Sam and his pals were then relieved and took shelter in a barn for the night. In a letter to Mr Bowker, his former headmaster, he said he was in the pink of condition, but that the nights 'and his feet', were very cold, and that some cigarettes would not go amiss.

Sam also wrote to his sister in Altrincham, thanking her for the parcel and 'the woollen helmet' she had sent to him. He went on to say that despite the frost, the cold and the wet, he and his pals were as 'happy as pigs in dirt'. Their trenches were in a very bad state and they had spent hours pumping the water out. Fortunately, they had been supplied with top boots and 'skin' coats which 'keep us as warm as toast'. He recounts the results of a bombardment on the enemy line to their front which 'blew the Germans to smithereens'.

/...

He said that they were in the trenches for 6 days on that occasion and that he and his pals very much looked forward to receiving letters and parcels. He explained that when parcels arrived they made a pile of the food so that everyone got a share. Dinners were good, he said, and he was becoming a first rate cook. Sam concluded this letter to his sister by telling her of his first fearful experience of 'Whizzbangs'* which screamed as they neared their target.

Mid-way through June Sam's father received a letter from the Battalion Chaplain saying that the 10th Cheshire's had been subjected to a horrendous bombardment. Many men from Northwich and District had been killed or were missing. Sam was reported missing on 21 May and was thought to have been amongst the dead buried in the trenches.

The Battalion War Diary gives the 10th's position on 21 May as 'In trenches near to St.Eloy'. It goes on to confirm the contents of the letter from the Battalion Chaplain:

During the morning trenches shelled. At 3.45 pm intense bombardment continued for four hours – most trenches destroyed. Large proportion of men killed or wounded. At 7.45 pm enemy attacked and took over our trenches with little resistance – most men having been killed or wounded in the bombardment. We counter-attacked at 2.0am on 22nd May and succeeded in retaking our lines. Casualties: 35 Killed, 106 Wounded, 41 Missing.

But Sam wasn't dead. Towards the end of June, and completely out of the blue, his father received a letter from Sam to say that he was a prisoner of war and that, although wounded slightly, he was being treated with 'the best of respect', by the enemy. Nonetheless, Sam died in captivity six months later. There is no record as to the cause of his death. His wound may have become infected or, he may have, like so many others, died of starvation.

Sam was held in captivity in the Douai area captured by the Germans from the French in October 1914. The area remained in enemy hands for the next four years. Douai Communal Cemetery was used during the occupation years for prisoners-of-war from many countries, as well as Germans killed close by. The inscription at the base of Sam Ashley's headstone reads 'He died as nobly as he lived'.

* 'Whizzbangs' German 77mm high velocity artillery shells which spent a very short time in flight.

Private Sam Ashley

Sam Ashley, Private No. 17829
10th Battalion, The Cheshire Regiment
Died while a prisoner of war, Monday 20 November 1916. Age 19
His is buried in Douai Communal Cemetery, Nord, France. A 31

Private Sam Ashley's Headstone in Douai Communal Cemetery

Private Sam Ashley

Sam Ashley's Awards

The 1914 –1915 Star

The British War Medal

The Victory Medal

Private Sam Ashley is also commemorated on the Moulton Methodist Church Tablet

In Sacred Memory
of
those connected
with this church and school,
who made the supreme sacrifice in the Great War
1914 – 1919.

ASHLEY SAM	FOSTER JACK	RAVENSCROFT GEO.
BUCKLEY ROBERT	GROVES HARRY	SHAW JOSEPH
BUCKLEY ROBERT H.	HITCHINSON HORACE	SOUTHERN JAMES
BUCKLEY WILMOT	HODKINSON HARRY	SOUTHERN THOMAS
CLARKE JERVIS	LUNT WILLIE	TOMLINSON DAN.
CLARKE WILLIAM J.	LUNT GEORGE	TOMLINSON ENOCH
COOKSON WILLIAM H.	MADDOCK JACK	TOMLINSON JOHN
CRANK JOHN	NODEN ARTHUR	WAKEFIELD PETER
DIDSBURY WALTER	PRICE ELIJAH	WEEDON GEORGE

The memorial tablet in Moulton Methodist Church.

Dedicated to the Memory of Robert H Buckley

Prior to the war Robert Buckley worked for a firm of boilermakers in Hyde, Cheshire and it was from here that he enlisted in the Cheshire Regiment. He was born at 57 Regent Street, Moulton in 1879. At the time of the 1881 Census (Aged 2) he was one of five children of Luke and Fanny Buckley. There were also two other children, Ruth and William Sparks, living in the small terraced house at that time.

In 1891 Luke, Robert's father, a Salt Boiler, is recorded as living at 24 Regent Street with his sons George and Robert. Also living with them was Ruth (nee Sparks) now married with a small daughter. A mystery surrounds the whereabouts of Fanny and her remaining three children. Maybe she was away visiting relatives at the time of the Census?

In July 1915 Robert's name appears on the Moulton Roll of Honour as serving in the 14th Battalion, the Cheshire Regiment. He was drafted to the front in September and around this time transferred ito the 11th Battalion.

The 3 July 1916 War Diary entry of the 11th Battalion states:

Attacked en-mass with Border Regiment on our left. Heavy machine gun fire took the Battalion out in lines. Survivors retreated back to their own trenches. Casualties: Every Company Commander, 10 other Officers, 307 other ranks. Of the 20 Officers and 657 other ranks who entered the trenches on 3rd July 6 Officers and 350 other ranks came out on the night of 4th

The Cheshire's Regimental History confirms the entry as follows:

... They were met by a withering fire of machine guns, under which they walked forward till the Battalion simply melted away. Colonel Aspinall was killed. Every Company Commander was a casualty. The Adjutant, Captain Hill, of the Suffolk Regiment, with great energy and bravery got the survivors back to the starting line. On the morning of the 4th, no organised body of men existed, 'one simply ran about no-man's land collecting men here and there' said one Officer ...

Robert was involved in the Battle of the Somme and in September his wife expressed grave concern that she had not heard from her husband for two months. Subsequently the War Office advised her that he had been killed in action on 3 July.

The body of Robert Buckley was never recovered and along with 72,000 others, his name is commemorated on the Thiepval. Memorial to the Missing. Robert was 37-years old when he died leaving a wife and three children to mourn his passing.

Private Robert H Buckley

Robert H Buckley, Private No. 15918
11th Battalion, The Cheshire Regiment
Killed in Action, Monday 3 July 1916. Age 37
His name is ommemorated on the Thiepval Memorial to the Missing
Somme, France
Pier and Face 3C and 4A

The Thiepval Memorial to the Missing, Somme, France

Private Robert H Buckley

Robert H Buckley's Awards

The 1914 –1915 Star   The British War Medal   The Victory Medal

Private Robert H Buckley is also commemorated on the Moulton Methodist Church Tablet

In Sacred Memory
of
those connected
with this church and school,
who made the supreme sacrifice in the Great War
1914-1919.

ASHLEY SAM	FOSTER JACK	RAVENSCROFT GEO.
BUCKLEY ROBERT	GROVES HARRY	SHAW JOSEPH
BUCKLEY ROBERT H.	HITCHINSON HORACE	SOUTHERN JAMES
BUCKLEY WILMOT	HODKINSON HARRY	SOUTHERN THOMAS
CLARKE JERVIS	LUNT WILLIE	TOMLINSON DAN.
CLARKE WILLIAM J.	LUNT GEORGE	TOMLINSON ENOCH
COOKSON WILLIAM H.	MADDOCK JACK	TOMLINSON JOHN
CRANK JOHN	NODEN ARTHUR	WAKEFIELD PETER
DIDSBURY WALTER	PRICE ELIJAH	WEEDON GEORGE

The memorial tablet in Moulton Methodist Church.

Dedicated to the memory of Robert Buckley

Bob Buckley enlisted in the Cheshire Regiment in January 1915. He was the fourth son of George and Ann Buckley and was one of thirteen children. When Bob was three-years old the family (numbering 11 at that time) lived at 5 Moulton Lane (Main Road). Ten years later they had moved to 1 Church Street. Fortunately, by then, the four eldest children had flown the nest, for there were now two additional mouths to feed. George ran the village newsagents and was well known throughout the village.

Bob was born in 1878 and, after leaving school, he worked at Brunner Mond's Alkali works at Winnington. He married Ellen and they had two children, George and Ann. He was a member of the local 'Odd Fellows' Lodge and attended the local Methodist Church. Bob would regularly treat his family to his rendering of 'The Old Rugged Cross' – his favourite hymn.

After enlisting in the Cheshire's he was listed in the Moulton Parish Roll of Honour in July 1915 as serving with the 14th Battalion. Later he transferred to the 10th Battalion and it was with this Battalion that he embarked for the front in December 1915.

On 12 July 1916, Bob was in action on the Somme in front of Ovillers, when a German shell exploded close by. He sustained terrible injuries including the loss of his arm. Two Moultoners, serving alongside him, Corporal Archie Whitlow of the Royal Army Medical Corps and Private Gilbert Ashton of the Machine Gun Corps went to his aid and saw him safely stretchered away to the nearest dressing station. From there he was transferred to No. 21 Casualty Clearing Station at La Neuville but died of his wounds on 15 July 1916. He was 39-years of age and the oldest man from the village to die in the war. At the end of July, the Battalion's War Diary lists the casualties for the month: 42 Killed, 75 Missing and 283 Wounded.

After the war, Bob's wife Ellen re-married. Her second husband was Mark Moore from Davenham.

Private Robert Buckley

Robert Buckley, Private No. 10/24614
10th Battalion, The Cheshire Regiment
Died of Wounds, Saturday 15 July 1916. Age 39
He is buried at La Neuville Cemetery, Corbie, Somme, France. I.B.34

Private Robert Buckley's Headstone in La Neuvelle Cemetery

Private Robert Buckley

Robert Buckley's Awards

The British War Medal   The Victory Medal

Other Memorials commemorating Private Robert Buckley's name

The memorial tablet in Moulton Methodist Church.

Private Robert Buckley

Brunner Mond War Memorial, Winnington.

Private Robert Buckley's bronze Memorial Plaque.

Private Robert Buckley

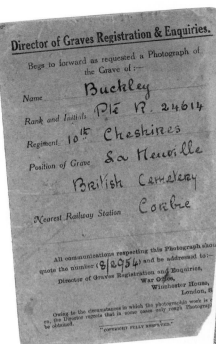

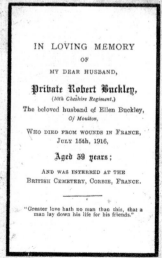

Above:
Request for an official photogtaph of
Private Buckley's grave.

Above right:
The photograph of Private Buckley's
grave marker.

Right:
A Memorial Card to Private Buckley
produced on behalf of his wife Ellen.

IN LOVING MEMORY
OF
MY DEAR HUSBAND,

Private Robert Buckley,
(10th Cheshire Regiment.)

The beloved husband of Ellen Buckley,
Of Moulton,

WHO DIED FROM WOUNDS IN FRANCE,
JULY 15th, 1916,

Aged 39 years;

AND WAS INTERRED AT THE
BRITISH CEMETERY, CORBIE, FRANCE.

"Greater love hath no man than this, that a
man lay down his life for his friends."

A group of the 10th Battaion The Cheshire Regiment showing Private Buckley on the extreme right holding a bowl

Dedicated to the Memory of Jervis Clarke

Before enlisting in Manchester in September 1914, Jervis Clarke worked in the Cooperage Department at Brunner Mond's Winnington works, where he fashioned casks for despatching Sodium Carbonate and other Alkali products to markets far and wide. On his marriage, just prior to the war, he left Moulton and set up home at 13 Church Road, Northwich. The young couple had one child. His widowed mother and sister remained in Moulton.

Jervis was a keen sportsman and could show most people a clean pair of heels. He ran for Castle Harriers and later took over the training of Jack Ashley, a well-known Moulton cyclist. He was a dedicated Christian and worked hard for his local Church. His two brothers also served in the army as did his brother-in-law.

He is mentioned in the 1915 Parish Roll of Honour as serving in the 7th Battalion, the East Lancashire Regiment. For reasons unknown, quite a few Moulton lads decided to serve in non-Cheshire battalions during the War.

On Sunday 30 July 1916, the 7th East Lancs., still part of the 19th Division, but temporarily attached to the 58th Brigade, were ordered to dig-in at Becourt Wood just south of La Boisselle, west of Albert. As they worked, the German artillery registered on them and put down a heavy bombardment.

Jervis's friend, Jack Kettle, who also lived in Church Road, was close to him when the shelling started and asked him if he could share his dug-out until things had quietened down. They talked as best they could with shells screaming overhead, and Jervis told Jack that he had spent the day bringing wounded in from the field.

During a lull in the barrage, Jack left the dug-out to go about his duties. Shortly afterwards a shell landed close by and a piece of shrapnel extinguished his life instantly. He was buried on the spot by his friends. They erected a marker cross over the grave but, as often happened, the grave was lost in the heat of battle. He is now commemorated on the Thiepval Memorial to the Missing .

The following day the 7th East Lancs. marched away from Becourt Wood to billets at Franvillers. During the period 19–31 July the Battalion lost 38 men killed and 95 wounded or missing.

Private Jervis Clarke

Jervis Clarke Private No. 6789
7th Battalion, The East Lancashire Regiment
Killed in Action, Sunday 30 July 1916. Age NK
His name is commemorated on the Thiepval Memorial to the Missing
Somme, France
Pier and Face 6C

The Thiepval Memorial to the Missing, Somme, France

Private Jervis Clarke

Jervis Clarke's Awards

The British War Medal   The Victory Medal

Other memorials commemorating Private Jervis Clarke's name

Northwich Town War Memorial

The memorial tablet in Moulton Methodist Church.

Brunner Mond War Memorial, Winnington

Dedicated to the Memory of Joseph Shaw

In 1891 a one-year old Joseph Shaw is recorded on the Census as living with his parents John and Mary Ellen Shaw and five other siblings at 3 Gleaves Lane, Moulton. By the early 1890s the family had moved to 3 School Lane, the family home for at least the next 25 years. John, a Salt Boiler, like many men from the village, worked for one of the numerous salt companies in the locality.

At five- or six-years old Joseph enrolled at the local council school in School Lane. From his home at No. 3 he could reach the school in less than a minute. After leaving school, he followed his father into the salt industry and took a job with Salt Union Ltd. Later he married a Winsford girl and they settled-down in Moulton.

At the outbreak of war, Joseph enlisted in the Cheshire Regiment and was initially drafted into the 14th Battalion. Later he transferred to the 13th Battalion, part of the 72nd Brigade, 25th Division. In the spring and summer of 1915 his name appeared on both the School and Parish Rolls of Honour. His brother George served with the Army in Salonica and it was whilst here that he learned of Joseph's death on the Somme – killed in action on 7 July 1916.

The Regimental History recalls the action:

The 13th Battalion, commanded by Col. L.H.K. Finch, was employed, on the 7th July, under the 12th Division against Ovillers. Jumping off trenches had been contrived from the newly won German trenches in La Boisselle… It had been arranged that the attack should be protected by smoke and by an intense barrage. But there was no smoke and our men thought the barrage particularly feeble. It is probable that, as the wind dropped, the smoke rose at once. Our advance, being thus unscreened, drew heavy artillery fire. This fire, together with machine gun fire from front and flanks, stopped the attack about half way to Ovillers.

The Battalion lost eight officers killed and twelve wounded, including their Commanding Officer, Colonel Finch. A total of 243 N.C.Os and other ranks were killed or wounded. Joseph Shaw was one of them. His body was never recovered from the field and his name is commemorated on the Thiepval Memorial to the Missing. He is in good company, for four others of the '34 Men' of Moulton are also remembered on this monument.

Private Joseph Shaw

Joseph Shaw, Private No. 124271
13th Battalion, The Cheshire Regiment
Killed in Action, Friday 7 July 1916. Age 26
His name is commemorated on the Thiepval Memorial to the Missing
Somme, France. Pier and Face 3C and 4A

The Thiepval Memorial to the Missing, Somme, France

Private Joseph Shaw

Joseph Shaw's Awards

The 1914 –1915 Star   The British War Medal   The Victory Medal

Other memorials commemorating Private Joseph Shaw's name

The memorial tablet in Moulton Methodist Church.

Private Joseph Shaw

Salt Union War Memorial, Winsford

Winsford Town War Memorial

St. Chads War Memorial,
Over, Winsford

Dedicated to the Memory John Tomlinson

Like a messenger of death, the telegraph boy peddled down Main Road on that autumn morning in 1916. Strapped to his belt was a leather pouch containing a most urgent message. As he passed by, people sent up their silent prayers "Please God – not our house". Amelia Tomlinson, John's mother, was tending the fire in her kitchen when the knock came.

In 1881 John Tomlinson's grandparents, John and Sarah, were living at 57 Moulton Lane (Main Road). At that time they had four children, including George, the eldest and father to be of John.

By 1891 George, aged 25, had met and married Amelia, who was then 18 and they lived at 37 Regent Street. George was a Salt Boiler and most probably worked the salt pans at the Newbridge Salt Works close to the village.

George and Amelia raised a family of four boys and two girls. John, the eldest, was born in June 1891. He attended Moulton Council School. By the outbreak of war he was married with three children, but took the King's shilling as soon as hostilities began. Some time before his death the family set up house at 4 Grange Hill, Winsford. John was posted to France in the summer of 1915. At about the same time he was listed on both the village and school Rolls of Honour as serving in the Durham Light Infantry.

Between 1 and 18 October 1916 the battle of Le Transloy was fought. On the 11th, men of the 2nd Battalion, the Durham Light Infantry took over Needle Trench to the south of Gueudecourt, a village south of Bapaume. On the 13th, the Battalion moved forward to occupy Rainbow Trench, east of the village.

At 5.15 am on 15th the Durham's quietly stood-to in their trenches and waited for the order to attack. As the whistles blew they scrambled 'over the top' and forward into No-Man's Land. To their front lay their objectives, the German held Mild and Cloudy trenches. At the end of the battle 3 officers and 19 NCOs and other ranks lay dead on the field. John Tomlinson was one of them. The attack failed and the 2nd Battalion limped back to Needle Trench to count their losses, re-group and prepare to fight another day.

John's body was never recovered and his name is inscribed on the Thiepval Memorial to the Missing. At the end of October 1916 the Durham Light Infantry's War Diary records that 142 officers and men were killed, wounded or missing during the month.

Private John Tomlinson

John Tomlinson, Private, Acting Lance-Corporal, No. 6488
2nd Battalion, The Durham Light Infantry
Killed in Action, Sunday 16 October 1916. Age NK
His name is commemorated on the Thiepval Memorial to the Missing
Somme, France
Pier and Face 14A and 15C

The Thiepval Memorial to the Missing, Somme, France

Private John Tomlinson

John Tomlinson's Awards

| The 1914 –1915 Star | The British War Medal | The Victory Medal |

Other memorials commemorating Private John Tomlinson's name

In Sacred Memory
of
those connected
with this church and school,
who made the supreme sacrifice in the Great War
1914–1919.

ASHLEY SAM	FOSTER JACK	RAVENSCROFT GEO.
BUCKLEY ROBERT	GROVES HARRY	SHAW JOSEPH
BUCKLEY ROBERT H.	HITCHINSON HORACE	SOUTHERN JAMES
BUCKLEY WILMOT	HODKINSON HARRY	SOUTHERN THOMAS
CLARKE JERVIS	LUNT WILLIE	TOMLINSON DAN.
CLARKE WILLIAM J.	LUNT GEORGE	TOMLINSON ENOCH
COOKSON WILLIAM H.	MADDOCK JACK	TOMLINSON JOHN
CRANK JOHN	NODEN ARTHUR	WAKEFIELD PETER
DIDSBURY WALTER	PRICE ELIJAH	WEEDON GEORGE

The memorial tablet in Moulton Methodist Church.

Private John Tomlinson

Salt Union War Memorial, Winsford

Winsford Town War Memorial

St. Chads War Memorial,
Over, Winsford

Whitegate St. Mary's War Memorial

Dedicated to the Memory of Joseph Henry Yardley

Joseph Yardley was born at 48 Dean Street, Over, Winsford in 1880. He was one of ten children of William and Mary Yardley. William was a Salt Boiler and worked for one of the salt refining companies in the area. Mary Yardley (née Latham) was a Moulton girl who had at one time lived at 69 Regent Street.

Having served in the Regular Army prior to the war Joseph, a reservist, was called-up as soon as hostilities began. He joined the Manchester Regiment and found himself posted to the 2nd Battalion. Four of Joseph's brothers also served.

The Battalion's War Diary states that the battalion left their billets at Senlis on the evening of 30 June 1916 and proceeded to Black Horse shelters at Crucifix Corner preparatory to going into action on the following morning. At 7.30 am the Battalion left Crucifix Corner and advanced along Dumbarton Track in Authuille Wood where they were placed in reserve along with the 15th Battalion, the Highland Light Infantry – the Glasgow Tramways Battalion.

At 1.45 pm two companies of the 2nd Manchester's fought their way towards the Leipzig Salient and entered the trench system. What they found there was heartbreaking. Highlanders, Borderers, Yorkshire Light Infantry, Lancashire Fusiliers and Dorsets were all in a sorry state. They had been subjected to artillery and machine gun fire for over six hours, while managing to repel counter-attacks from enemy bombers advancing along their own trenches. Dead and dying men where everywhere, with hundreds lying close up on the unbroken enemy wire.

During the afternoon the Manchester's, along with men from other battalions, fought their way forward. Prisoners were taken and made to run the gauntlet of their own fire on their way back to the British positions.

By the end of the day the 32nd Division had lost nearly 4,000 officers and men dead, wounded or missing (33% of the Division's strength). Lying among the carnage in No-Man's Land alongside many of his friends from the 2nd Battalion, Manchester Regiment, was the body of Acting Corporal Joseph Henry Yardley of Moulton. His body was never recovered. He was 36-years old.

Private Joseph Henry Yardley

Joseph Henry Yardley, Private, Acting Corporal, No. 2328
2nd Battalion, The Manchester Regiment
Killed in Action, 1 July 1916. Age 36
His name is commemorated on the Thiepval Memorial to the Missing
Somme, France
Pier and Face 13A and 14C

The Thiepval Memorial to the Missing, Somme, France

Private Joseph Henry Yardley

Private Joseph Yardley's Awards

The 1914 –1915 Star   The British War Medal   The Victory Medal

---

Private Joseph Henry Yardley is also commemorated on the Moulton Methodist Church Tablet

In Sacred Memory
of
those connected
with this church and school,
who made the supreme sacrifice in the Great War
1914 – 1919.

Ashley Sam	Foster Jack	Ravenscroft Geo.
Buckley Robert	Groves Harry	Shaw Joseph
Buckley Robert H.	Hitchinson Horace	Southern James
Buckley Wilmot	Hodkinson Harry	Southern Thomas
Clarke Jervis	Lunt Willie	Tomlinson Dan.
Clarke William J.	Lunt George	Tomlinson Enoch
Cookson William H.	Maddock Jack	Tomlinson John
Crank John	Noden Arthur	Wakefield Peter
Didsbury Walter	Price Elijah	Weedon George

The memorial tablet in Moulton Methodist Church.

Passchendaele Ridge in October 1917

1917

A YEAR OF PROMISE

IT WAS 'ALL QUIET ON THE WESTERN FRONT' at the start of 1917. No major battles were fought in January or February. Both sides were content to let the worst winter of the war pass and to try to survive the mud, cold and wet as best they could. The usual trench activities went on, of course, fortifications were improved, wire was replaced, patrols ventured into No-Man's Land at night, guns and mortars spat out their occasional messages of death, and snipers searched behind their sights for the unwary.

On 1 February Germany made a serious error of judgement when they declared 'unrestricted' U-boat warfare on ships of any country aiding the Allies. This eventually provoked President Wilson of America into abandoning his policy of neutrality, and declaring war on the Axis powers. America would need 12-months to attain war readiness and to be of use to the Allies in France or Belgium. However, the mere fact that they had climbed off the fence, gave a great moral boost to the Allies. On the other hand, the Axis powers felt that by cutting-off British sources of supply they could finish them before the Americans were ready to take the field.

On 12 March an event took place which would colour the history of the remainder of the 20th century – the Russian revolution began.

Also in March, German High Command made a strategic decision to abandon their long-held trench lines of 1914–1916 and to retire some 25 miles to their newly constructed Hindenburg Line. Before re-positioning they carried-out a 'scorched earth' policy of blowing bridges, roads and railway stations, firing property and poisoning wells and reservoirs.

During the six months between April and October the French, occupying the line to the right of the British from Chemin des Dames to the Swiss frontier, were subjected to bouts of indiscipline and mutiny in their infantry regiments. Some troops refused point-blank to return to the line. The majority, however, were prepared to occupy the trenches, but not to advance against the German guns. Petain, the new French

The wounded... Australian wounded outside a captured German pillbox converted to a dressing station

Commander-in-Chief, gradually won over the trust of his men with a mixture of strong discipline and good leadership. Of 23,000 troops charged with the crime of mutiny, 50 or so were eventually executed.

Early April saw major battles around Arras, the River Scarpe and Vimy. The Canadians, using medieval caves and tunnels opened by British Royal Engineers' Tunnelling Companies were able to move their men in complete safety to the line in front of Vimy ridge prior to their attack. The enemy, not expecting an offensive until the end of the month, were taken completely by surprise with their crack reserve troops held too far in the rear to be of any use. The Canadians took Vimy Ridge and looked down, for the first time, on the Douai plain beyond.

The defeat at the Battle of Arras caused the Germans to sack their chief of staff and followed this some days later by giving Faulkenhousen, their General Officer Commanding, his marching orders too. By mid-May, having captured over a mile of the front Hindenburg Line trenches, the battle was wound down. Net result was a frontage gain of 20 miles to a depth of 5 miles. Total Allied casualties were approximately 160,000 killed, wounded or missing. German casualties amounted to about the same with over 20,000 prisoners taken.

On the 21 May a heavy bombardment started, continuing until 7 June, pre-empting the opening of the Battle of Messines. In what is accepted as the best planned and implemented assault of the war, up to 2,000 guns firing 3.5 million shells were used to break German resolve. At 3.10 am on the 7th, just 30 minutes before dawn, 19 deep-dug mines comprising 450 tons of ammonal were triggered below German strongpoints on the eastern and southern slopes of the Messines Ridge, stretching from Hill 60 in the north to St. Yves in the south, effectively clearing the ridge of all resistance. Vibrations were even felt on the south coast of England. Unlike the Somme a year earlier, the bombardment, coupled with the mines, did their work well. There was little or no desire to fight left in a dazed and demoralised foe as nine British and Empire divisions took over the ridge and the ground beyond. The Battle of Messines cleared all risk of observation and prevention from the south of the Ypres Salient by the enemy of what was to be 1917's major offensive to the north – the Third Battle of Ypres. Opening on 31 July, Third Ypres constituted in fact eight battles covering the period from 31 July to 10 November – the Battles of Pilckem, Langemarck, the Menin Road, Polygon Wood, Broodseinde, Poelcappelle, First Passchendaele and Second Passchendaele

The dead... German dead outside their gun emplacement near Zonnebeke, Belgium

These in turn became known as the Battles for Passchendaele, a name that still brings-to-mind carnage and suffering endured under the worst conditions imaginable. From August onwards the weather around the Ypres Salient was foul. Drainage systems were eliminated, river banks were destroyed, shellholes filled with water and trenches became mud-filled ditches. Metalled roads had been shelled out of existence and plank roads and walkways substituted. To stray from these man-made paths was to court oblivion. Again the curse of the troops, trench foot, returned with a vengeance. Men stood for days up to their knees in water and mud in footwear which just could not cope with the conditions.*

The Battles for Passchendaele ended with the British, breaking out of the Salient, and in control of the ground well beyond the German 1st, 2nd and 3rd line trenches. No fewer than 51 British and Dominion divisions and 78 German divisions were involved. The cost to the British and her Dominions was 49,611 killed, 232,292 wounded and 29,068 missing.

A measure of the fighting can be judged by the award of 59 Victoria Crosses during the Battles for Messines and Passchendaele.

To the south of Arras in northern France lies the town of Cambrai where the last major battle of 1917 took place. This time however, as well as the infantry, tanks would be employed en-mass. The ground selected by the Tank Corps was considered most suitable for these mechanical monsters, weighing up to 30 tons each. At 6.20 am on 20 November, and without the usual bombardment, upwards of 300 of them lumbered forward. The enemy was taken completely by surprise and, within four hours, the Hindenburg Position had been taken. Regrettably, the break in the German line was not fully exploited due mainly to poor leadership, inadequate preparation, a shortage of reserves and a war-weary force, most of whom had been fighting since Third Ypres. Momentum was lost and stalemate followed.

The year ended with the Russians, now in the midst of building a Bolshevik State under Lenin and Trotski, suspending hostilities against the Central Powers. This enabled Germany to move over 30 Divisions from the east to west. Allied prospects for the New Year now looked grim.

*Authors Note: One soldier serving in the salient with the 1/7th Worcester Regiment was so badly affected by trench foot that he was hospitalised to Hexham in Northumberland where he recovered. He was then posted to the Italian Front to fight against the Austrians until the end of hostilities. He was Private Joseph Leonard Crompton – my dad… GAC.

Gun emplacements in a 'wood' in Zillebeke, Belgium – known as Sanctuary Wood

Other Fronts

In the Balkans battles for Lake Prespa took place throughout March and April, with another three battles for Isonzo taking place on the Italian front. Renewed activity in Palestine saw battles at Gaza, Jaffa and Jerusalem which fell to the British in December. In April the Germans moved out of East Africa. In Mesopotamia the British were successful against the Turks at Kut and saw the fall of Baghdad. At sea the U-boat war was stepped up a peg and German destroyers shelled Margate and Broadstairs. In May the Dover Patrol bombed Zeebrugge.

Moulton

In the Vestry minutes for April, Mr Proudlove, with much feeling, praised those men of the Church who had gone forth to fight. Later the Vicar thanked Mr R Hitchinson for all the hard work he had put in with the choir. His son, Horace Hitchinson, would later die in India, three weeks before the end of the war in Europe.

In June, Sir Joseph Verdin wrote to a Mrs Hammerton of Regent Street, asking for an updated list of men serving in the armed forces. He wished to send them all a gift of tobacco. This act of kindness was a regular feature of his interest and affection for the village.

At the end of October a concert was arranged in the Verdin Institute to swell the coffers of the Red Lion's Soldiers' and Sailors' Patriotic Fund. Artists taking part were Gunner H Gunson, of the Principal Lancashire Concerts, aided by Misses Meakin, Stelfox, Cooper and Leese. Mr Percy Moffit, a comic and a Moulton favourite, also took part. A house-to-house collection in November in aid of the Moulton Soldiers and Sailors Christmas Fund raised £20. This brought the total to £52.

News from the front in 1917 brought much grief to the population of Moulton. No fewer than seven of its manhood were to give their lives that year. They were **Fred Bates, Harry Hodkinson, Jack Maddock, George Ravenscroft, Thomas Southern, Enoch Tomlinson** and **Albert Walker.**

A 'Tommy's-eye-view' of a sector of the Hindenburg Line

Dedicated to the Memory of James Freederick Bates

As James Bates closed the door on his little lock-up Grocers shop in Moulton in April 1916, he little knew that it would be for the last time. Some days later he enlisted at Winsford in 'A' Company, 22nd Battalion, the Manchester Regiment. Four months later, in August, he was drafted to the Western Front were he served until his death some 9-10 months later. He was 36 years old. His older brother, Oswald, who had enlisted during the early days of the war, was wounded at the outset of the war and discharged.

James was the youngest son of Fredrick and Hannah Bates who, in 1881, were resident at 45 New Road, Over, Winsford. At that time they had three children, 10-year old John B , 8-year old Gertrude J and 2-year old Oswald L. Fred's father was an Engineer at Messrs Bates Foundry, also in New Road, Winsford.

Although 35 years of age in 1916, James was unmarried and lived with his brother John and his wife Emily at 'Westwood', Crook Lane, Winsford. Towards the end of April 1917 James wrote two letters, one to his sister-in-law Emily in which he appeared very cheerful, and one to his brother John. In this, his last letter, he enclosed a sum of money, explaining that 'He thought it would be safer with them'. He ended his letter by wishing them goodbye!

On 21 May 1917, 2nd Lieutenant Jackson of the Manchester's, wrote from near Arras to say that over five days had elapsed since their last attack and that James had not been seen since. He went on to explain that sometimes, in the heat of battle, men became separated from their units and fought alongside others until they could be re-united with their own Battalion. Sometimes, he continued, men were adrift for a week or more and it was for this reason that he had not written sooner. Jackson concluded by saying that he now feared the worst and that James had been killed in the initial attack on 13 May.

/...

The Battalion War Diary of the 13th states:

In line at Bullecourt – South East of Arras. At 3.40 am 'A' & 'D' Companies carried out an attack on the 'Redpatch' in conjunction with the 2nd Royal Warwick's who attacked from the South West. 'A' & 'D' Companies attacked from the North East with bayonets fixed. 'B' Company attached to the 1st South Staffs. 'C' Company remained in railway embankment. Our own barrage inflicted severe casualties on 'A' & 'D' Companies. German strong points engaged 'A' & 'D' Company and Royal Warwick's with machine gun fire and they were forced to dig in. Sniper fire heavy during the day. 'A' & 'D' Companies returned to their own trenches at dusk. Attack failed because of the inaccuracy of our own barrage. Casualties: 109 Killed, Wounded or Missing.

The body of James Frederick Bates was never recovered and his name is commemorated on the Arras Memorial to the Missing. This huge Memorial, designed by Sir Edward Lutyens, carries the names of 35,000 men of the British and Commonwealth Forces who died between the Spring of 1916 and August 1918 and have no known grave.

Private James Freederick Bates

James Frederick Bates, Private No. 40760
22nd Battalion, The Manchester Regiment
Killed in action, Sunday 13 May 1917. Age 36
His name is commemorated on the Arras Memorial and
Faubourg d'Amiens Cemetery, Pas de Calais, France. Bay 7.

The Arras Memorial and Faubourg d'Amiens Cemetery, Pas de Calais, France

Private James Freederick Bates

James Frederick Bates' Awards

The British War Medal   The Victory Medal

Other memorials commemorating Private James Frederick Batess name

Winsford Town War Memorial

Private James Freederick Bates

Christ Church War Memorial,
Wharton, Wimsford

St. Chads War Memorial, Over,
Winsford

Dedicated to the Memory of Harry Hodkinson

Harry Hodkinson, born at 71 Regent Street, Moulton in 1887, was the fifth son of Thomas and Mary Hodkinson. His father was a bricklayer and in the 1891 Census is credited with having eight children including Harry, then 3-years old. From that point on little, if anything, is known about Harry. At some time prior to 1914 Harry married a Moulton girl, Sarah Jane, and moved to Barnton, Northwich. After the start of the war, Harry left his job with Brunner Mond Ltd to enlist at Northwich. He joined the 3rd Battalion, the Cheshire Regiment.

In November 1915 Lance-Corporal William Hodkinson, one of Harry's older brothers, in a letter to Mr Bowker, headmaster of Moulton Council School, said that he was serving with the 10th Cheshire's and that they were having a hard time of it. Writing from his dugout he said that his Company were part way through a second spell in the trenches and that the conditions were appalling. He went on to describe how thousands of rats and mice plagued them during the night, living off anything they could find, including the dead bodies of soldiers in No-Man's Land. Houses and the Church in the nearby village had been flattened by German artillery and he complained of the severe cold which chilled him and his friends to the bone. He and his pals were very much looking forward to having a go at the enemy .

According to the Regimental History the 3rd Cheshire's were designated a Special Service battalion. On mobilisation in 1914, the Battalion proceeded to its war station in Birkenhead. Liverpool and Birkenhead became 'a Defended Port' and the Garrison was know as Mersey Defences. The duties of the Cheshire's were to guard the Docks and other strategic positions around the Wirral. By end 1915 its strength was over 3,000 men.

Harry was taken ill in August 1917 and died in an Auxiliary Hospital at Wallasey. The illness he suffered and died from is a mystery. His funeral took place on 30 August and he was laid to rest in St. Winifrid's cemetery, Davenham. The inscription at the base of his headstone reads 'At Rest'.

Although a resident of Barnton his name does not appear on the Barnton Parish Church Tablet. His wife, Sarah Jane, re-married after Harry's death and became Mrs Weston. She settled with her new husband in Workington, Cumberland.

Private Harry Hodkinson

Harry Hodkinson, Private No. 64780
3rd Battalion, The Cheshire Regiment
Died at home, Sunday 26 August 1917. Age 30
He is buried in St Wilfred Churchyard Davenham. Old 31.

Harry Hodkinson's headstone in St Wilfred Churchyard, Davenham

Private Harry Hodkinson

Harry Hodkinson's Awards

The 1914–1915 Star   The British War Medal   The Victory Medal

Other memorials commemorating Private Harry Hodkinson's name

In Sacred Memory
of
those connected
with this church and school,
who made the supreme sacrifice in the Great War
1914–1919.

ASHLEY SAM	FOSTER JACK	RAVENSCROFT GEO.
BUCKLEY ROBERT	GROVES HARRY	SHAW JOSEPH
BUCKLEY ROBERT H.	HITCHINSON HORACE	SOUTHERN JAMES
BUCKLEY WILMOT	HODKINSON HARRY	SOUTHERN THOMAS
CLARKE JERVIS	LUNT WILLIE	TOMLINSON DAN.
CLARKE WILLIAM J.	LUNT GEORGE	TOMLINSON ENOCH
COOKSON WILLIAM H.	MADDOCK JACK	TOMLINSON JOHN
CRANK JOHN	NODEN ARTHUR	WAKEFIELD PETER
DIDSBURY WALTER	PRICE ELIJAH	WEEDON GEORGE

The memorial tablet in Moulton Methodist Church.

Brunner Mond War Memorial, Winnington.

Dedicated to the Memory of Jack Maddock

On arrival in Belgium on 6 September 1917 as a Pioneer in the 11th Battalion, the Prince of Wales Volunteers (South Lancashire Regiment), Jack Maddock was transferred into the 7th Battalion forming part of the 19th Division, 56th Brigade. Two weeks later he was dead – killed in action in the Ypres Salient – he was 19 years of age.

Jack was the son of George and Sarah Maddock of Regent Street, Moulton and, before joining the armed forces, worked for Messrs. Russel Allen of Davenham Hall. He was born in Moulton in 1896 and had two brothers serving in the forces: George in the Transport Section of the 10th Cheshire's and Herbert in the Transport Section of the Royal Field Artillery. George was wounded in 1916 and Herbert was on his way to France or Flanders when Jack met his death.

On that fateful day, the Brigade was in reserve in dug-outs on the side of the Ypres–Comines Canal. The 7th Battalion was located on the north bank and to the west of a pontoon bridge between Spoil Bank and The Bluff. As the rest of the brigade assaulted the enemy line some members of the 7th Battalion were detailed-off to help as stretcher-bearers to carry wounded from the field. Jack was one of the men detailed and it was whilst performing this duty that a shell landed close by killing him instantly.

The body of Jack Maddock was never recovered from the battlefield and his name is recorded on the Memorial at Tyne Cot, West Flanders, Belgium. Tyne Cot Memorial is the largest of all the Commonwealth War Grave Cemeteries.

It took it's name from the British soldiers' spelling and pronunciation of the local Flemish dialect for '*het hennekot*' (hen or chicken houses) with the commom local usage of '*het*' as '*t*' and the silent '*h*', hence '*t'hennekot*' *(t'ennekot)*.

In early November 1917 a Service to the memory of Jack Maddock was held at the Primitive Methodist Church. The Reverend G Emmett officiated.

Private Jack Maddock

Jack Maddock, Private No. 29431
7th (11th) Battalion, The South Lancashire Regiment
Killed in action, Thursday, 20 September 1917. Age 19
His name is commemorated on the Tyne Cot Memorial
Zonnebeke, West Flanders, Belgium. Panel 92 to 93 and 162A

The Tyne Cot Memorial, Zonnebekke, West Flanders, Belgium

Private Jack Maddock

Jack Maddock's Awards

The British War Medal   The Victory Medal

Private Jack Maddock is also commemorated on the Moulton Methodist Church Tablet

In Sacred Memory

of
those connected
with this church and school,
who made the supreme sacrifice in the Great War
1914–1919.

ASHLEY SAM	FOSTER JACK	RAVENSCROFT GEO.
BUCKLEY ROBERT	GROVES HARRY	SHAW JOSEPH
BUCKLEY ROBERT H.	HITCHINSON HORACE	SOUTHERN JAMES
BUCKLEY WILMOT	HODKINSON HARRY	SOUTHERN THOMAS
CLARKE JERVIS	LUNT WILLIE	TOMLINSON DAN.
CLARKE WILLIAM J.	LUNT GEORGE	TOMLINSON ENOCH
COOKSON WILLIAM H.	MADDOCK JACK	TOMLINSON JOHN
CRANK JOHN	NODEN ARTHUR	WAKEFIELD PETER
DIDSBURY WALTER	PRICE ELIJAH	WEEDON GEORGE

The memorial tablet in Moulton Methodist Church.

Private Jack Maddock

Jack Maddock's Memorial Card

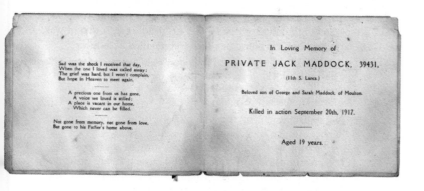

Sad was the shock I received that day,
When the one I loved was called away;
The grief was hard, but I won't complain,
But hope in Heaven to meet again.

A precious one from us has gone.
A voice we loved is stilled;
A place is vacant in our home,
Which never can be filled.

Not gone from memory, not gone from love,
But gone to his Father's home above.

In Loving Memory of

PRIVATE JACK MADDOCK, 39431,

(11th S. Lancs.)

Beloved son of George and Sarah Maddock, of Moulton.

Killed in action September 20th, 1917.

Aged 19 years.

Dedicated to the Memory of George Ravenscroft

There are few references in the archives to George Ravenscroft. According to the 1881 Census his mother and father, Edward and Hannah, lived with their three daughters (aged 11, 9 and 1) at 5 Maddocks Lane, Moulton. Edward was a Salt Boiler with one of the local Salt Companies. By 1891 the family had moved to 50 Main Road, Moulton and young George was now on the scene, aged four. By this time the eldest daughter, Edith (aged 21) had flown the nest. By 1896 the family were living at 68 Main Road and it was in this house that they remained for the next 25 years.

On leaving school George secured a job with Salt Union Ltd and it was whilst working for this company that he joined the Royal Field Artillery sometime into the war. The date of his enlistment is unknown, but as his name is not present on either the School or Parish Rolls of Honour for May and July 1915, it can be surmised that he joined up sometime towards the end of 1915 or even in 1916.

After serving with the RFA, George was transferred to the Loyal North Lancashire Regiment. It was whilst serving with the regiment's 8th Battalion that he met his death. The Battalion War Diary describes the action in which George died as follows:

9/10 July 1917 – Battalion in line at Hooge Sector, Ypres.
18 July 1917 – Raid carried out by 100 men of 'C' Company on 'Ignorance Trench'. Objectives to destroy the trench and capture prisoners for intelligence purposes.

When the men of the 8th Loyal North Lancs. entered 'Ignorance' Trench they found it deserted. A devious enemy had flown the coop and, as a welcome to the North Lancs. they shelled their own front line and support lines causing many casualties amongst the British troops. Aside from 23 men dead and wounded a total of 11 men did not answer their names at roll call after the attack. George Ravenscroft was one of them. He was 21-years old.

George is one of 17 Moulton men whose bodies were never accorded a proper Christian burial. His name, as with a number of other Moulton men, is commemorated on the Menin Gate Memorial at Ypres, Belgium.

Private George Ravenscroft

George Ravenscroft, Private No. 28034
8th Battalion, The Loyal North Lancashire Regiment
Killed in action, Friday 20 July 1917. Age 20
His name is commemorated on the Menin Gate Memorial,
Ypres, West Flanders, Belgium. Panels 41 and 43

The Menin Gate Memorial, Ypres, West Flanders, Belgium

Private George Ravenscroft

George Ravenscroft's Awards

The British War Medal   The Victory Medal

Other memorials commemorating Private George Ravenscroft's name

The memorial tablet in Moulton Methodist Church.

Private George Ravenscroft

Salt Union War Memorial, Winsford

Dedicated to the Memory of Thomas Southern

Thomas Southern was 21 years of age when he was killed in action on Saturday 17th February 1917. He was born on 29 December 1895, the son of Peter and Eliza Southern (née Garner), who lived successively in Main Road and School Lane, Moulton, at the turn of the century. Later on the family left Moulton to live at Weaver Street, Winsford. Thomas had at least three other siblings, James, Rachel and Eliza. On leaving school he secured employment as a boxmaker with Salt Union Ltd.

After his wedding Thomas and his new wife rented a house at Bradford Mill Cottages, Meadow Bank. In June 1916 he presented himself for enlistment under the 'Derby' scheme at Winsford and found himself a member of the Cheshire Regiment. At first Thomas served with the 14th Battalion but later transferred to the 10th forming part of the 7th Brigade, 25th Division. He enjoyed a last leave in October 1916 before saying goodbye to his wife and marching off into oblivion.

The Battalion War Diary for 1917 records that on 17 February whilst occupying trenches at Ploegsteert, one officer and 65 other ranks were ordered to raid the German lines next to Factory Farm. During the attack the Cheshire's bombed the German dugouts inflicting many casualties. They destroyed bomb dumps and equipment and took ten prisoners. Unfortunately, eight of these men were killed by their own 'friendly' machine gun fire as they crossed No-Man's land towards the British lines.

It was during this attack that Thomas Southern lost his life. He was first wounded in the arm whilst fighting in a German trench and ordered back to his lines to receive attention. As he approached the haven of his own trenches he was mortally wounded in the head by a bullet fired from behind. Platoon Sergeant Collins, in a letter to Mrs Southern, said that he and Thomas had been the best of friends, both in and out of the line, and that Thomas was a good soldier. He expressed his deepest sympathy.

Sadly, lightning does sometimes strike twice in the same place. In December 1918 James Southern, serving with the 2nd Cheshire Regiment, and Thomas's elder brother, died of wounds in Salonika. His grave is in the Mikra British Cemetery in Greece.

Private Thomas Southern

Thomas Southern Private No. 44284
10th Battalion, The Cheshire Regiment
Killed in action, Saturday, 17 February 1917. Age 21
His name is commemorated on the Ploegsteert Memorial
Comines-Warneton, Belgium. Panels 4 and 5.

The Ploegsteert Memorial, Comines-Warneton, Belgium.

Private Thomas Southern

Thomas Southern's Awards

The British War Medal   The Victory Medal

Other memorials commemorating Private Thomas Southern's name

In Sacred Memory of those connected with this church and school, who made the supreme sacrifice in the Great War 1914-1919.

Ashley Sam	Foster Jack	Ravenscroft Geo.
Buckley Robert	Groves Harry	Shaw Joseph
Buckley Robert H.	Hitchinson Horace	Southern James
Buckley Wilmot	Hodkinson Harry	Southern Thomas
Clarke Jervis	Lunt Willie	Tomlinson Dan.
Clarke William J.	Lunt George	Tomlinson Enoch
Cookson William H.	Maddock Jack	Tomlinson John
Crank John	Noden Arthur	Wakefield Peter
Didsbury Walter	Price Elijah	Weedon George

The memorial tablet in Moulton Methodist Church.

Private Thomas Southern

Winsford Town War Memorial

Salt Union War Memorial, Winsford

St. Chads War Memorial, Over, Winsford

Dedicated to the Memory of Enoch Tomlinson

Enoch Tomlinson was born at 23 Regent Street on 5 October 1893. His parents Isaac (25) and Fanny (24) already had one daughter, Emma (2), when he arrived in this world. Fanny originated from Winnington, Northwich, Isaac from Moulton. He was a Salt Boiler with one of the local salt companies.

On leaving Moulton Council School, he took a job with Salt Union Ltd. In 1926 this company, along with Brunner Mond, merged with other manufacturers to form the great Imperial Chemical Industries (ICI). As a teenager Enoch played football for Northwich Vics., was well known locally as an outstanding outside right, renowned for his speed and dribbling skills. He was a fine looking young man and very popular with the ladies. His sweetheart in early 1916 was Lily Gandy, a Moulton girl.

In Northwich, on 18 May 1916, Enoch enlisted in the Royal Garrison Artillery. Later he would transfer to the Royal Horse/Royal Field Artillery, 57th Trench Mortar Battery. Before leaving for France, Enoch gave Lily a gold and ruby 'Friendship' ring. He said that he hadn't bought an engagement ring for he had a funny feeling that he might not return. This ring is still treasured by Lily's aunt, Beryl Lumsden, who still lives in the village.

In a letter dated 1 May 1917, Enoch's sister received the following news from the Assistant Matron at Wimereux Hospital, France:

Dear Miss Tomlinson, I am very sorry to have to tell you that your brother died in this hospital at 4.45pm on 30th April 1917. He passed quietly and peacefully away and was unconscious at the end. He was very badly wounded and died as a result of his wounds. With Sympathy, Yours Sincerely ......(Illegible) Asst. Matron.

Enoch was 23 years old when he died at Wimereux Hospital. He is buried in the communal cemetery there and is in good company. The poet, Lieutenant-Colonel John McCrae who wrote *In Flanders Fields,* lies close by.

According to the Electoral Rolls Isaac was still living at 23 Regent Street in 1919. There is no mention of his wife Fanny.

Isaac, Enoch's father, had the following inscribed on his son's headstone.

Gone but not forgotten
From Dad, Brothers and Sisters

Gunner Enoch Tomlinson

Enoch Tomlinson, Gunner No. 4202850
57th Trench Mortar Battery, Royal Field Artillery, Royal Horse Artillery
and Royal Garrison Artillery
Died of wounds, Monday 30 April 1917. Age 23.
Buried at Wimereux Communal Cemetery, Pas de Calais, France. II.J.5

Enoch Tomlinson's Headstone in Wimereux Communal Cemetery,
Pas de Calais, France.

Gunner Enoch Tomlinson

Enoch Tomlinson's Awards

The British War Medal   The Victory Medal

Other memorials commemorating Gunner Enoch Tomlinson's name

In Sacred Memory
of
those connected
with this church and school,
who made the supreme sacrifice in the Great War
1914–1919.

ASHLEY SAM	FOSTER JACK	RAVENSCROFT GEO.
BUCKLEY ROBERT	GROVES HARRY	SHAW JOSEPH
BUCKLEY ROBERT H.	HITCHINSON HORACE	SOUTHERN JAMES
BUCKLEY WILMOT	HODKINSON HARRY	SOUTHERN THOMAS
CLARKE JERVIS	LUNT WILLIE	TOMLINSON DAN.
CLARKE WILLIAM J.	LUNT GEORGE	TOMLINSON ENOCH
COOKSON WILLIAM H.	MADDOCK JACK	TOMLINSON JOHN
CRANK JOHN	NODEN ARTHUR	WAKEFIELD PETER
DIDSBURY WALTER	PRICE ELIJAH	WEEDON GEORGE

The memorial tablet in Moulton Methodist Church.

Gunner Enoch Tomlinson

Salt Union War Memorial, Winsford

Enoch Tomlinson's Memorial Card

For His Country

In Loving Remembrance of

Gunner Enoch Tomlinson,

Who died of wounds received in action whilst fighting in France, on April 30th, 1917.

Aged 23 Years

Into the field of battle
He bravely took his place,
He fought and died for England
And the honour of his race.
He sleeps not in his native land
But neath a foreign sky,
Far from those who love him best
In an Hero's grave he rests.

115

Dedicated to the Memory of Albert V Walker

Just after war was declared, the brothers Walker, Harold and Albert (Bert), made their way to the Recruiting Office in Northwich and signed up for the duration. Harold was posted to the Cycle Corps and Albert to the Cheshire Regiment. They were the sons of Mr and Mrs G Walker of Mayfield Cottage, Main Road, Moulton.

Both boys were born in Moulton and attended the local Council School, a stones throw away from their home. In May 1915 they were included in the School's Roll of Honour. On leaving school, Bert secured a prestigious a job in the laboratory of Brunner Mond & Company at Winnington. He was also a chorister and sang in the church choir at St. Stephens.

As soon as Bert completed his initial training he qualified as a machine gunner and was attached to one of the four companies which made up the 10th Battalion. Soon afterwards the Battalion became part of the 7th Brigade, 25th Division, and ordered to the Western Front.

In November 1915 one of Bert's pals, writing to his uncle at Lodge Farm, Moulton said that he and his brother, Sydney Proudlove, had met up with both Harold and Bert Walker at rest camp. They had shared a few beers and swapped stories about their life back in the village. He went on to say that he thought that Harold Walker had been drafted to the Serbian Front.

On 16 February 1917 Albert Walker was manning a trench near Ploegsteert when a shell exploded near by. A fragment of the shell found its mark and Albert was evacuated to the nearby casualty clearing station. He died the same day of his wounds. He was 19-years old.

On 6 April 1917 the Reverend J C Turner conducted a memorial service to Bert Walker in front of a packed congregation in St. Stephens.

Private Albert V Walker

Albert V Walker Private No. 13591
10th Battalion, The Cheshire Regiment
Died of wounds, Friday, 16 February 1917. Age 19
He is buried in Bailleul Cemetery Extension, Nord, France. III.A.38

Albert Walker's headstone in Bailleul Cemetery Extension, Nord, France.

Private Albert V Walker

Albert Walker's Awards

The 1914–1915 Star	The British War Medal	The Victory Medal

Other memorials commemorating Private Albert Walker's name

In Sacred Memory
of
those connected
with this church and school,
who made the supreme sacrifice in the Great War
1914-1919.

Ashley Sam	Foster Jack	Ravenscroft Geo.
Buckley Robert	Groves Harry	Shaw Joseph
Buckley Robert H.	Hitchinson Horace	Southern James
Buckley Wilmot	Hodkinson Harry	Southern Thomas
Clarke Jervis	Lunt Willie	Tomlinson Dan.
Clarke William J.	Lunt George	Tomlinson Enoch
Cookson William H.	Maddock Jack	Tomlinson John
Crank John	Noden Arthur	Wakefield Peter
Didsbury Walter	Price Elijah	Weedon George.

The memorial tablet in Moulton Methodist Church.

Brunner Mond War Memorial, Winnington.

German infantry on their way through Ploegsteert Wood, Belgium during their spring offensive in 1918

1918

Defeat Into Victory

A T THE START OF 1918, German High Command saw a window of opportunity that would inflict a crippling blow that would lead to victory. With extra divisions released from the eastern front it would take advantage of its superior numbers before the untried Americans could take the field. Time was of the essence, for its policy of unrestricted U-boat activity had failed against newly devised 'convoy' systems. Ludendorff decided to hit British lines from Arras to St. Quentin with his 'Operation Michael'. He knew that, with the British defeated, he could deal with the French at his leisure. On the night of 20 March, after a short bombardment, his troops attacked *en-mass*. Despite heroic efforts by the defenders their lines were breached. On the first day both sides suffered some 40,000 casualties. In addition, the British lost over 500 guns. Of the 40,000 British casualties over 21,000 became prisoners of war.

In the days following, the Germans re-took the old battlefields of 1916. Their advance however was not without difficulty, for the quality of these troops left much to be desired. Within two weeks 'Operation Michael' had shot its bolt and was stopped some 10 miles short of Amiens.

Between 9 and 29 April, Ludendorff made another attempt to break through with his 'Operation Georgette'. Over 20 days, battles raged at the River Lys, Estaires, Messines, Hazebrouk, Bailleul, Kemmel, Bethune, and the Scherpenberg. At first the Germans made good progress against demoralised troops of the Portuguese 2nd Division at Neuve-Chapelle. They followed this by capturing Messines village and some of its now infamous ridge. Appeals by Haig to the French for reinforcements fell at first, on stoney ground. Haig then issued his now famous Order of the Day to try to lift his tired and weary troops:

There is no other course open to us but to fight it out. Every position must be held to the last man. There must be no retirement. With our backs to the wall and believing in the justice of our cause each one must fight to the end. The safety of our homes and the freedom of mankind alike depend upon the conduct of each one of us at this critical moment.

The arrival of two fresh British divisions and the 1st Australian Division eased the situation, but the retreat continued. Passchendaele Ridge, taken at such cost in October 1917, was forfeited for better positions to the east of Ypres. In Picardy, preceded by a mixed bombardment of explosive and mustard gas shells, German tanks broke through on a three mile front and captured Villers-Bretonneux. It was during this fight that the first tank versus tank battle took place. That night, Rawlinson took the initiative and let the 13th and 15th Australian Brigades off the leash. The Aussies, supported by the British 18th and 58th Divisions, stormed back into Villers-Bretonneux. Despite further small advances the enemy had run out of steam leaving Ludendorff no option but to call-off the offensive.

In Britain at the end of April, the age of conscription was raised from 41 to 50 – indicating clearly that Britain was running out of men. In June, Spanish flu began to sweep through the ranks of the German Army, helped by their poor physical state.

Having soaked up all that the Germans could throw at them in March and April, it was the turn of the Allies to go on the offensive. Haig, planned

Time for a cup of tea ...

and executed a brilliant campaign which brought the German Army to it's knees. At 4.20 am on 8 August the British 4th Army, attacked over the old killing fields of the Somme, quickly taking the German 1st, 2nd and 3rd line beyond. Australian and Canadians pushed forward for eight miles taking guns and prisoners as they went. At the end of the day the German Army was in disarray, losing over 27,000 men. Ludendorff later wrote that 8 August 1918 was the blackest day in the history of the German Army.

Despite opposition from the French General Foch, Haig insisted that his 3rd Army should be used to outflank the Germans, and was fully vindicated by the success of this plan, bringing the German Army to the brink of despair. On 11 August, a severely mauled Ludendorff offered to resign. The Kaiser refused, but accepted that the end was near, and that Germany must search for a way out. Over the next three months the pace of events quickened with German determination crumbling in the face of relentless pressure from the Allies. Losses were heavy on both sides as Allied troops punched holes in the German lines from the Channel to Verdun. At the end of September the Hindenburg Line was breached and

... and a smoke

German resolve was fast running out ...

German resolve was fast running out. They knew they could no longer hope to salvage anything other than an 'honourable' peace. They were tenacious to the end, and fought no less hard as they retreated, than had the BEF in their retreat from Mons in 1914. In October, as the advance continued, a series of diplomatic notes were handed to Germany, the third demanding unconditional surrender, leaving no honourable exit for the Germans. Certainly its front line troops could not accept that they had been defeated – they were still occupying enemy soil. Time would prove that the 'disgrace' of unconditional surrender, would generate a canker of hate in the hearts of many Germans, not the least of whom, was a moustachioed Bavarian infantry corporal, wounded south of Bapaume in 1916 and gassed in Flanders in 1918 – one Adolf Hitler. Kaiser Wilhelm II abdicated in early November and was accepted into exile by the Dutch.

The terms of the Armistice were signed in a railway carriage near Retondes in the Forest of Compiegne at 5.05 am on 11 November 1918. The main requirements were: 1) Germany, with immediate effect, was to evacuate all occupied territory, including Alsace-Lorraine; 2) The Allies would occupy all German territory up to the Rhine (and did so until June 1930); 3) Germany would surrender huge quantities of arms including all U-boats; 4) The German fleet was to be disarmed and interned.

At 11.0 am on the 11th day of the 11th month, peace reigned.

Other Fronts

Whilst the activity on the Western Front dominated, war was still being waged in other lands. Battles were fought from Mesopotamia to India. British Forces fought numerous battles in Palestine finally capturing Sidon, Beirut and Aleppo in October. In Italy the Allies got the upper hand at Piave and were the first of the Allies to set foot on enemy territory when they marched into Austria in early November. After many reverses and fierce fighting the Turks finally surrendered after the British occupied Mosul in early November. The British Navy still controlled the seas and, in April, a fleet of over 70 vessels successfully landed an assault force at the German U-boat base at Zeebrugge, took the heavily defended 'mole' and rendered the base unusable by blocking the approach canal with naval hulks. On the other hand, sailors of the German High Seas Fleet, knowing that further resistance was futile, refused to take their ships to sea.

The railway carriage in which the Armistice was signed

Moulton

New Years eve saw a concert and supper dance at the Verdin Institute in aid of the Red Lion's Soldiers and Sailors Patriotic Fund. The founder and secretary of the fund, Mr Joseph Winstanly led the team that made the arrangements and bookings. The concert party was the Winnington New Stars Pierrot Troop and the dance orchestra was led by Mr Prests. £20 was raised for the Fund.

At a committee meeting of the Soldiers and Sailors Christmas Comforts Fund, in February, the Vicar, Reverend J C Turner took the chair. The treasurer, Mr J Winstanly, said that £101.16s.0d had been raised over the year. After making grants to men serving at the front, it was decided to subscribe five shillings each to those men of the village who had received their discharge after serving overseas. In addition a subscription of £5 was allocated for local prisoners-of-war.

June saw the departure from the village and St Stephen's of Reverend J C and Mrs Turner to take up a new living at Ravenstone Dale, Westmorland. During his ministry he saw the erection of the Church Hall. In August the new vicar Reverend J T Vale MA was instituted.

Because of the influenza epidemic sweeping the country and indeed the world, the headmaster of the Council School, Mr H W Bowker* was forced to close the school from July to January 1919.

Although war's end, and the long-awaited peace in 1918 was celebrated in Moulton as it was throughout the country, it was a year for grieving for many in the community.

Another 12 men of Moulton had lost their lives in the last year of the conflict. **Corporal Arnold Buckley, Leading Seaman William Henry Cookson, Private Walter Didsbury, Corporal John William Foster, Private Harry Groves, Private Horace Hitchinson, Private John William Jones, Private Oliver Middleton, Private James Southern, Second-Lieutenant Dan Tomlinson, Private Peter Wakefield** and **Private Arthur Frederick Wilkinson** were to make the supreme sacrifice in that year of Allied victory.

Mr Harold Walter Bowker served as Headmaster of the village Council School from 1910 to 1922. He lived, with his wife Ann, at 'Elia', Jack Lane, Moulton.

British troops crossing the Hohenzollern Bridge into Cologne, November 1918

Dedicated to the Memory of Arnold Buckley

Arnold Buckley was born in Middlewich in 1892. Before then his parents, James and Mary, lived at 52 Princess Street, Wharton, Winsford. James was a Salt Boiler. On his marriage to his sweetheart Elizabeth, Arnold settled in Moulton and it was from here, in March 1915, that he enlisted into the Cheshire Regiment.

In July 1915 Arnold is shown on the Moulton Roll of Honour as serving in the 3rd Battalion.. Usually a regiment's 3rd Battalion was restricted to either training duties at base HQ or 'Special Reserve' duties in the immediate locality. Later in 1915 he was drafted to the front with the 1st Battalion and served continuously in at least two theatres of war for three years. He was promoted to the rank of Corporal and was never far away from the sharp end of the conflict. During his service he was wounded three times and gassed once, which succinctly sums up the kind of war he experienced. The Regimental History reads:

> On the night of 20/21st August, the Battalion marched to its assembly position west of Bucquoy... Starting just before dawn, under a heavy barrage, the infantry advance began in pitch darkness and a heavy ground mist, which made co-operation and maintenance of direction very difficult. Bucquoy and the second objective were swiftly taken, hostile outposts being completely taken off guard, and offering little resistance...

> Achiet was captured without very heavy casualties by 'A' and 'B' Companies, which with 'C' Company, pushed on through the village to the final objective, the railway line. 'D' Company was left to mop up a large number of prisoners, a battery of artillery, and many machine guns. As the Battalion debouched from the village, the fog lifted and the leading companies... 'came under heavy machine gun fire from beyond the railway and from both flanks. But this did not stop them from fighting their way up the hill, reaching the railway line, and holding it...' the usual determined counter-attack was made, mainly on the left flank, and was successfully repulsed.

The Battalion went into action 600 strong and lost no less than 300 killed and wounded on this day, three officers being killed and eight wounded. The Battalion was relieved in the evening. Arnold Buckley was one of those killed in this attack.

Just before he was killed on 21 August 1918 Arnold spent 14 days at home on leave with his family. The body of Arnold Buckley were never recovered from the battlefield and his name is commemorated on Vis-en-Artois Memorial at Pas de Calais. Arnold had three other brothers serving. One was badly wounded early on in the war and discharged, the other two survived to tell their children and grand children about their experiences.

Corporal Arnold Buckley

Arnold Buckley, Corporal No. 25674
1st Battalion, The Cheshire Regiment
Killed in action, Wednesday 21 August 1918. Age 26
His name is commemorated on the Vis-en-Artois Memorial
Pas de Calais, France. Panel 16

The Vis-en-Artois Memorial, Pas de Calais, France

Corporal Arnold Buckley

Arnold Buckley's Awards

The 1914 –1915 Star   The British War Medal   The Victory Medal

Other memorials commemorating Private Arnold Buckley's name

St. Chads War Memorial
Over, Winsford

Corporal Arnold Buckley

Christ Church War Memorial, Wharton, Wimsford

Dedicated to the Memory of William Henry Cookson

At the end of his short leave, William Cookson kissed his wife Millie and his 4-year old daughter, Annie, and said his goodbyes. He asked them to wave him off from outside 23 Regent Street, Moulton which they shared with Millie's uncle, Isaac Tomlinson and his family. As he held his wife he whispered that he had a 'funny' feeling that he would not be coming back. When he reached the junction with Main Road he turned and saluted them. It was the last time they would see him alive. Two weeks later, on 20 January 1918, he lay, with 12 of his shipmates, at the bottom of the English Channel. His ship, *H.M.S Mechanician*, was torpedoed by a German U-Boat, some eight miles off St. Catherine's Point on the Isle of Wight. William was 31-years old.

Born in 1886, he was the son of William and Ann Cookson of 28 Alan Street, Northwich. He joined the Royal Navy and, on completing his service, was placed on the Naval Reserve. He married Millie Tomlinson and they settled in Moulton Village where they had one child – Annie. He worked for the River Navigation Trustees as a diver until called-off the Reserve on 6 August 1914. He was the very first of 230 Moulton men to march off to war.

His naval record shows time served aboard His Majesty's Ships, *Calliope, Andromeda, Sutlej, Amphritite, Rinaldo, Minotaur* and finally *Mechanician*. After his time serving on *Amphritite* he was trained as a gunner at Devonport, before joining *Rinaldo*, a coastal ship.

Towards the end of 1914, *H.M.S. Minotaur*, with Wiliam aboard, was involved in the bombardment of the Belgian coast inflicting heavy punishment on the German coastal defences there. In it's turn, *Minotaur* was attacked by coastal guns, air ships and submarines, eventually taking direct hits before limping to nearby Dunkirk to disembark her wounded. She then took course to Dover for repair and refit before returning to shell Zeebrugge for another four days. William recounts how his gun layer, standing beside him, was struck by a piece of shell which went in at the knee and out at the ankle.

/...

In July 1915, William's name appeared on the Moulton Village Roll of Honour and showed him serving again in *Rinaldo*. Sometime in mid-1917 he joined *Mechanician* a former cargo liner.

January 1918 was a traumatic month for the Cookson family. William was lost on the 20th and his younger brother, Herbert, serving with the 12th Battalion, Cheshire Regiment, was killed 10 days later whilst fighting in Macedonia. His remains are interred in Doiran Military Cemetery, Greece, close to the Yugoslav border.

After the death of William, Millie received £149.3s.7d from her husband's estate. Annie eventually married Leslie Carter from Meadow Bank and they settled at 23 Regent Street, Moulton. Their only daughter Glenys now lives in Haverfordwest, Pembrokeshire.

As with most of the '34' there remain unanswered questions. In the case of William, there is a question mark as to why his name appears on both the Winsford Town War Memorial and also that of St. Chads, Over, Winsford. In Ann Clayton's book 'A Cheshire Parish at War', written in dedication to the men whose names appear on St. Chads War Memorial, William's home address is given as 148 Dingle Lane, Winsford. This is a mystery to both Glenys Clarke (Millie's grand-daughter) and the rest of her family. It may well be that Millie and her daughter, Annie, went to live with a relative for a short while after William's death and before she married Leslie Carter and moved back to 23 Regent Street, Moulton.

Leading Seaman William Henry Cookson

William Henry Cookson, Leading Seaman/Acting Petty Officer
SS/582 (RFR/DEV/B/2690). Royal Navy
H.M.S. Mechanician
Killed in action, Sunday 20 January 1918. Age 31
His name is commemorated on the Naval War Memorial, Devon. Panel 26

The Naval War Memorial, Devon.

Leading Seaman William Henry Cookson

William H Cookson's Awards

The 1914 –1915 Star   The British War Medal   The Victory Medal

---

Other memorials commemorating Leading Seaman William Cooksons name

In Sacred Memory
of
those connected
with this church and school,
who made the supreme sacrifice in the Great War
1914–1919.

Ashley Sam	Foster Jack	Ravenscroft Geo.
Buckley Robert	Groves Harry	Shaw Joseph
Buckley Robert H.	Hitchinson Horace	Southern James
Buckley Wilmot	Hodkinson Harry	Southern Thomas
Clarke Jervis	Lunt Willie	Tomlinson Dan.
Clarke William J.	Lunt George	Tomlinson Enoch
Cookson William H.	Maddock Jack	Tomlinson John
Crank John	Noden Arthur	Wakefield Peter
Didsbury Walter	Price Elijah	Weedon George

The memorial tablet in Moulton Methodist Church.

Leading Seaman William Henry Cookson

Winsford Town War Memorial

Northwich Town War Memorial

St. Chads War Memorial Over, Winsford

Leading Seaman William Henry Cookson

William Cookson's name remebered on the headstone of his wife in St. Wilfred Churchyard, Davenham

William Coockson's Memorial Card

For His Country

In Loving Remembrance of

LEADING SEAMAN

WILLIAM HENRY COOKSON,

DROWNED AT SEA, THROUGH SINKING OF
H.M.S. MECHANICIAN, JAN. 20TH, 1918,

AGED 31 YEARS.

"Little we thought his time so short
In this world to remain,
When from his home he went away,
And thought to come back again.
We do not know what pain he bore,
We did not see him die,
We only know he went away
And could not say Good bye."

Telegrams —" Navy Accounts, London."

In any further communication on this subject, please quote

No. 9. N.P. 783/18

and address letter to—
The Accountant General of the Navy,
Admiralty,
London, S.W.

Admiralty,

28 January, 1918.

Madam,

I regret to have to inform you that H.M.S. " *Mechanician* "

was sunk on the *20th instant* and that the name of

William Henry Cookson,

Rating *Leading Seaman* Official Number SS 582 , who is believed

(RFR Dev. B 2690)

to have been on board, does not appear in the lists of survivors received in

this department. In these circumstances it is feared that, in the absence

of any evidence to the contrary, he must be regarded as having lost

his life.

Any application which the next of kin or legal representative may

have to make in consequence of the foregoing information should be made

by letter addressed to the Accountant General of the Navy, Admiralty,

London, S.W, *except applications relative to Pension which should be addressed as directed in the attached leaflet.*

I am, *Madam,*

Your obedient Servant,

Accountant General of the Navy.

Mrs Millie Cookson,
23, Regent Street,
Moulton,
Nr Northwich,
Cheshire.

The telegram informing William Cookson's family of his death

Dedicated to the Memory of Walter Didsbury

Walter Didsbury and his older brother George enlisted together at Northwich at the outbreak of war. In 1915 their names were recorded on both the Parish and Council School Rolls of Honour as serving with the 12th Battalion, the Cheshire Regiment. They were born at 9 Regent Street, Moulton and were the sons of George and Mary Didsbury. Walter was born in 1890 and George in 1888.

Before taking the King's shilling Walter was employed as a chauffeur by Messrs I Robinson and Sons of Northwich. In September 1915 he was posted to France and there he remained until wounded in the right shoulder in May 1916. He was immediately sent for treatment at Cheltenham Hospital and later spent some time at home recovering to full fitness. He was transferred to the 12th Battalion and posted to Salonica. Coincidentally, his brother George, was also transferred into the same battalion at more or less the same time.

Whilst on a short leave in August 1918, George decided to take the plunge and married his sweetheart Charlotte Ashworth. After a brief honeymoon he re-joined his regiment in Macedonia.

The History of the Cheshire Regiment in Macedonia, carries a full account of the battle in which the 12th Battalion took part, and in which Walter Didsbury lost his life. It reads:

> The military situation on the Struma (River) was one of stalemate for nearly two years... On August 8th 1918, the decision was taken by the Higher Command to put into operation the plan of a Serbian strategist, Voivode Nischitch.... on the front held by the British troops. 'P' Ridge, the strongest natural fortress in Europe was of predominant importance, and it was well know to both sides that the fall of this ridge would immediately be followed by the invasion of Bulgaria...
>
> The attack began on September 15th and by the night of the 16th six Serbian divisions and one cavalry division were pouring through the gap made on 15th... The Bulgarian Army were cut in two.... After four days preliminary bombardment and wire cutting, the 66th Infantry Brigade, led by the 12th Battalion (Cheshire Regiment), attacked the Ridge... At 'zero', eight minutes past 5 am, the Battalion advanced to attack the formidable whale-backed ridge several hundred metres high...

Then followed a detailed account of the attack which goes on to say that the preliminary gas bombardment had little effect and that the artillery were unable to make any impression on the strong dug-outs of the enemy. 'A' Company fought their way into the enemy trenches where severe hand to hand fighting took place. Colonel Clegg-Hill then led an attack on the next ridge but was checked by the detonation of a bomb dump causing many casualties and confusion. Heavy machine gun fire coupled with a barrage of trench mortars and flame-throwers made the going very, very difficult. In the face of this onslaught the Battalion pressed home their attack and stormed their objective. Colonel Clegg-Hill was now mortally wounded and assisted to a shell hole to be looked after by a medic.

The enemy then counter-attacked with machine guns. The enfilading fire was merciless, 'B' and 'C' Companies were annihilated. So severe was the cross fire that nothing could survive in the area. The 12th Battalion simply ceased to exist and somewhere among the dead lay Walter Didsbury. He was 28-years old. Some 50 or 60 survivors withdrew to Jackson's ravine where the remnants of the Brigade were reorganised. Casualties: 8 Officers killed including the Commanding Officer, Colonel Clegg-Hill, 10 Officers wounded, 274 other ranks killed, wounded or missing.

The 12th Battalion was led away from the action by the only unwounded officer. By 23 September the Bulgarian Army was in full retreat and pursued by other units of the British Salonica Force. For their gallant conduct The 12th Battalion was awarded the Croix de Guerre by the French.

On 16 May 1919 a Memorial Service was held for Walter Didsbury in the Primitive Methodist Church in Moulton where he had served as a Sunday school teacher. Walter's wife Charlotte opened a confectioners business in Station Road, Northwich. Later, she married Walter's friend and best man, Edward Alcock. They had one daughter, Sarah (Sally) who was born in October 1920.

Private Walter Didsbury

Walter Didsbury, Private No. 13954
12th Battalion, The Cheshire Regiment
Killed in action Thursday, 19 September 1918. Age 28
He is buried in Doiran Military Cemetery, Greece. VI.E.2

Walter Disdbury's headstone in Doiran Military Cemetery, Greece

Private Walter Didsbury

Walter Didsburyy's Awards

The 1914 –1915 Star   The British War Medal   The Victory Medal

Other memorials commemorating Private Walter Didsbury's name

In Sacred Memory
of
those connected
with this church and school,
who made the supreme sacrifice in the Great War
1914 – 1919 .

ASHLEY SAM	FOSTER JACK	RAVENSCROFT GEO.
BUCKLEY ROBERT	GROVES HARRY	SHAW JOSEPH
BUCKLEY ROBERT H.	HITCHINSON HORACE	SOUTHERN JAMES
BUCKLEY WILMOT	HODKINSON HARRY	SOUTHERN THOMAS
CLARKE JERVIS	LUNT WILLIE	TOMLINSON DAN.
CLARKE WILLIAM J.	LUNT GEORGE	TOMLINSON ENOCH
COOKSON WILLIAM H.	MADDOCK JACK	TOMLINSON JOHN
CRANK JOHN	NODEN ARTHUR	WAKEFIELD PETER
DIDSBURY WALTER	PRICE ELIJAH	WEEDON GEORGE

The memorial tablet in Moulton Methodist Church.

Private Walter Didsbury

Northwich Town War Memorial

Private Walter Didsbury

George and Charlotte Didsbury

Dedicated to the Memory of John (Jack) William Foster

Regrettably, there is very little written locally about the life of John (Jack) William Foster. Maybe this is because, at the time of his death, he lived at Newbridge, some distance from Moulton Village.

The 1891 Census records Jack (aged 1) living with his parents, Herbert and Harriet, at 74 Regent Street, Moulton along with his two sisters Sarah (aged 1) and Lilly (2 months). Harriet certainly wasted no time in having her babies – three in well under three years is pretty smart going. Herbert earned his living as a Salt Boiler, possibly at the Newbridge Salt Works.

At some time Jack went to live in Newbridge. However, there is no record as to whether this move was to accompany his parents or because of his marriage. What is certain is that at the start of hostilities, he enlisted at Northwich in the 2nd Battalion, Prince of Wales' Volunteers (South Lancashire Regiment). This battalion became part of the 75th Brigade, 25th Division.

Jack served on the Western Front and was promoted to the rank of Corporal. The Battalion War Diary for early April 1918 mentions that they are in billets in the Ypres Salient at Le Bizet and Rosignol Camp, Nieppe. During the early morning of 10 April, information was received that British lines were under sustained attack at Ploegsteert. At 9.30 am orders were received to move forward to positions 2,000 yards west of Ploegsteert. Battalion HQ was set up at Regina Farm.

At 11.30 am about 100 stragglers of the 8th Border Regiment came in and were deployed alongside the South Lancs. At 5 pm the Battalion were ordered to attack and to re-take Ploegsteert village. The attack failed and, during the assault, Jack Foster lost his life. His body was never recovered from the battlefield and his name is commemorated on the Ploegsteert Memorial to the Missing. He is in good company for there are 11,000 others who were also lost during the conflict and have no known graves. Jack Foster was 28-years old.

Corporal John (Jack) William Foster

John (Jack) William Foster, Corporal No. 31471
2nd Battalion, the South Lancashire Regiment
Killed in action, Wednesday, 10 April 1918. Age 28
His name is commemorated on the Ploegsteert Memorial
Comines-Warneton, Belgium. Panel 6 and 7.

The Ploegsteert Memorial, Comines-Warneton, Belgium

Corporal John (Jack) William Foster

John (Jack) William Foster's Awards

The 1914–1915 Star   The British War Medal   The Victory Medal

Corporal John (Jack) William Foster's name is also
commemorated on the Moulton Methodist Church Tablet

The memorial tablet in Moulton Methodist Church.

Dedicated to the Memory of Harry Groves

There is very little documented about the life of Harry Groves. The Electoral Rolls for 1919 show Harry's wife Alice living with her children, at 46 Main Road, Moulton. Before the war Harry worked for Salt Union Limited, most likely in the local Salt Mine, or at the Newbridge Salt Works.

Harry enlisted in the Cheshire Regiment early on and was posted to the 9th Battalion. In July 1915 he is shown on the Moulton Parish Roll of Honour as serving in the 3rd Cheshire's which, more than likely, was their training battalion.

Sometime before hostilities drew to their close, on the morning of 11 November 1918, Harry was severely wounded and taken to one of three General Hospitals at Le Treport, Seine-Maritime. It was here in the care of the nursing staff, that he died of his wounds on 14 November 1918, three days after the Armistice had been signed. The Regimental History recounts the 9th Battalion's actions between 2–7 November as follows:

> The 9th Battalion went into the line in front of Sommaing (due north of Le Cateau) on 2–3 November. The enemy, having withdrawn, the two leading companies pushed forward to regain touch (with them). They came under fire from machine guns near Jenlain… The whole front was subjected to bombardment. A platoon of the 9th Battalion managed to get into Jenlain. This made the enemy withdraw… All these movements were carried out not only under hostile but also under 'friendly' artillery fire.
>
> On the 4th, the attack on Jenlain was resumed under a barrage, which again caused some casualties to our men…. On the 7th, the 9th Battalion took part in an attack by the 57th Brigade on Bellignies. All objectives were gained, but the war diary had a great deal to say about our artillery barrage which made the attack 'very difficult and dangerous proceeding'. Our casualties (over this period) were nine officers wounded, 12 men killed and 132 wounded.

His wife Alice had the following inscribed on his headstone:

Gone but no forgotten
From his dear wife
and children

Private Harry Groves

Harry Groves, Private No. 25054
9th Battalion, The Cheshire Regiment
Died of wounds, Thursday, 14 November 1918 Age NK
He is buried in Mont Huon Military Cemetery
Le Treport, Seine-Maritimes, France. X.A.3A

Harry Groves' headstone in Mont Huon Military Cemetery
Le Treport, Seine-Maritimes, France

Private Harry Groves

Harry Groves' Awards

The 1914 –1915 Star   The British War Medal   The Victory Medal

Other memorials commemorating Private Harry Groves' name

In Sacred Memory
of
those connected
with this church and school,
who made the supreme sacrifice in the Great War
1914 – 1919.

ASHLEY SAM	FOSTER JACK	RAVENSCROFT GEO.
BUCKLEY ROBERT	GROVES HARRY	SHAW JOSEPH
BUCKLEY ROBERT H.	HITCHINSON HORACE	SOUTHERN JAMES
BUCKLEY WILMOT	HODKINSON HARRY	SOUTHERN THOMAS
CLARKE JERVIS	LUNT WILLIE	TOMLINSON DAN.
CLARKE WILLIAM J.	LUNT GEORGE	TOMLINSON ENOCH
COOKSON WILLIAM H.	MADDOCK JACK	TOMLINSON JOHN
CRANK JOHN	NODEN ARTHUR	WAKEFIELD PETER
DIDSBURY WALTER	PRICE ELIJAH	WEEDON GEORGE

The memorial tablet in Moulton Methodist Church.

Salt Union War Memorial, Winsford

Dedicated to the Memory of Horace Hitchinson

Generally, when people write about the Great War, they write of the Western Front and Gallipoli. Little is said of other fronts, and of the men of the British and Commonwealth who were killed and maimed in those forgotten fields. Battles raged throughout the world in the Balkans, Caucasus, Italy, Palestine, Mesopotamia, Africa and India and it was in India, during the 3rd Afghan War, that Horace Hitchinson died for his King and country.

The son of Richard Columbus and Charlotte Elizabeth Hitchinson of 17 Main Road, Moulton, he was born on 22 August 1892. Richard was a blacksmith and, prior to his marriage, lived in Church Street. Before setting up home in Main Road the family lived successively at 8 Kennerleys Lane and 66 Main Road. Before Horace appeared on the scene in 1892 the family totalled seven.

In his last year at Moulton Council School Horace was punished for 'Inattention to work' – 2 strokes of the cane. On leaving school he joined Brunner Mond Ltd and went to work at its Winnington site in Northwich. When war was declared, he responded to Lord Kitchener's appeal and enlisted at Winsford in the 8th Battalion, the Cheshire Regiment, the first Cheshire battalion to be raised in Kitchener's 'New Army'.

After his initial training, during the first half of 1915, Horace found himself on board *HMS Ivernia* heading for Gallipoli. After 8 monthsof fighting the Turks, and with little or nothing to show for it, the Allied Expeditionary Force stole away and into the night of 9 January 1916. On re-organisation, the battalion sailed for India and more confrontation – this time it was against the Afghans.

The Third Afghan War claimed the lives of 1,810 British soldiers in the Great War. Horace Hitchinson was one of them. He died 20 days before the Armistice was signed. He was 26-years old. It is not known how Horace died, however he was not killed in action. It may well be that he died of wounds, sickness or accident.

His name is commemorated on the Kirkee War Memorial, India. Regrettably, many troops who died, including Horace, are buried in civil and cantonment cemeteries around India and Pakistan where their graves can no longer be properly maintained.

The Committee of the Verdin Institute in Church Street, wrote a letter of condolence to Richard and Charlotte. Richard, was a member of the Institute and had served on the Management Committee for some years. In 1919 Richard and Charlotte moved back to 66 Main Road.

Private Horace Hitchinson

Horace Hitchinson, Private No. 3/64818
8th Battalion, The Cheshire Regiment
Died on Tuesday, 22 October 1918. Age 26.
His name is commemorated on the Kirkee 1914–1918 Memorial, India. Face 4.

The Kirkee 1914–1918 Memorial, India.

Private Horace Hitchinson

Horace Hitchinson's Award

The British War Medal   The Victory Medal

Other memorials commemorating Private Horace Hitchinson's name

The memorial tablet in Moulton Methodist Church.

Brunner Mond War Memorial, Winnington.

Dedicated to the Memory of John William Jones

John William Jones, a Liverpudlian, was a proud son of that great seaport and little or nothing can be found about him in the Moulton local press, school or parish records.

He was employed at Helsby Wire Works and married Eleanor Jones, also of Liverpool, around 1911. They lived with Eleanor's parents, Mr and Mrs Robert Swan, at 36 Regent Street, Moulton.

John enlisted in Liverpool during the early stages of the war. with the 18th King's Liverpool (2nd Liverpool Pals). In late 1915 the battalion sailed for France and was involved in the Battle of the Somme on 1 July 1916. The Scousers occupied the line North of Maricourt and close to the right flank of the British line. In fact they were the fourth Battalion along from the French with the 4th Manchester's on their right and the 8th East Surreys on their left. It was Captain Nevill of the 8th East Surreys who, when he kicked a football towards the German line at 7.30 am on that fateful day, wrote his name into the folklore of the Great war.

At the beginning of April 1918 the Germans launched their final, despairing attack, on the Allied lines. Operation 'Georgette' nearly succeeded. However, the tenacity and bravery of the British and Commonwealth troops repulsed the Germans and from then on they were on a slippery slope to capitulation.

On 28 April 1916 remnants of the 18th Kings, who had been severely knocked about earlier in the month, were furiously assaulted by the German infantry. Bravely they managed to hold the line, but at a cost, for it is now believed that during this scrap John William Jones received his fatal injuries. John was taken to a nearby Casualty Clearing Station where he succumbed to his wounds on 30 April. He was 27-years old.

Sadly, a note on John's file at the Commonwealth War Graves Office indicates that John's wife, Eleanor, living at 59 Hoole Road, Chester, died shortly after him.

Private John William Jones

John William Jones, Private No. 23056
18th Battalion, the The King's (Liverpool Regiment)
(2nd Liverpool Pals)
Died of wounds, Tuesday, 30 April 1918 Age 27.
He is buried in Esquelbecq Military Cemetery, Nord, France. I.B.21.

John William Jones' headstone in Esquelbecq Military Cemetery, Nord, France.

Private John William Jones

John William Jones' Awards

The 1914–1915 Star

The British War Medal

The Victory Medal

Dedicated to the Memory of Oliver Middleton

In the days when policemen pounded the beat in the dead of night, P.C. Bailey of Leftwich had been on his for over five hours when, at 3.45 am on 13 February 1915, while looking forward to breakfast and a warm bed, he spotted a cyclist riding along London Road without lights. As it neared him he stepped-out of the shadows giving 16-year old Oliver Middleton, an engine cleaner from Moulton, quite a shock His excuse was that he had filled his lamp with fuel when he set off, but it had leaked-out through a hole in the bottom. After feeling the lamp and finding it stone-cold, P.C. Bailey charged Oliver who appeared in front of the magistrates at Northwich Police Court some 10 days later. He was fined 2s.6d. Three years on, his young life was extinguished while attacking a small village in the north of France.

He was a bright young man. In summer 1910, in standard VI at Moulton Council School, he was awarded a £5 book prize for his good work. Born on 11 January 1899 he lived with his parents at Hillside Farm on the outskirts of Moulton. Sometime later the family moved into the village to live at 12 Chapel Street.

Oliver enlisted at Northwich and joined the 5th Battalion, the Cheshire Regiment. Later he was transferred to the 1st Battalion, Somerset Light Infantry. His name was recorded on both the School and Parish Rolls of Honour in 1915.

On 14 April 1918, his battalion was ordered to take the village of Riez Du, northeast of Loos, attacking at 6.30 pm from a position on the La Bassée Canal. The Battalion War Diary records:

The village will be taken at all costs, and every man in the Battalion will be used to obtain this object if necessary....

... 6.30pm – in position north of the Canal. Creeping barrage started. Very accurate machine gun fire by Germans – advance held up. Captain Osborne MC led two Companies in rushes at the enemy machine guns. Aided by our artillery and machine guns, troops entered the village and house to house fighting took place. Many Germans dead. Germans counter attacked on the Eastern outskirts of the village but were beaten back. Whole objective achieved.

It was during this action that Oliver Middleton lost his life.

After the war Oliver's father lived in Walsall, Staffordshire.

Authors note:

If Oliver Middleton's date of birth (18 January 1899) is correct then in April 1918 he would have been 19-years old, not 20 as recorded in the official records and on his grave. Additionally, as his name is shown on both the School and Parish Rolls of Honour in May and July of 1915 he could only have been 16 when he convinced the recruiting Sergeant at Northwich that he was old enough to accept the King's shilling. A very brave young man.

Private Oliver Middleton

Oliver Middleton, Private No.204781
1st Battalion, Prince Albert's (Somerset Light Infantry)
Killed in action Sunday, 14 April 1918. Age 20.
He is buried in Mont-Bernanchon British Cemetery
Gonneham, Pas de Calais, France. I.B.3.

Oliver Middleton's headstone in Mont-Bernanchon British Cemetery
Gonneham, Pas de Calais, France.

Private Oliver Middleton

Oliver Middleton's Awards

The British War Medal   The Victory Medal

Oliver Middleton's name is also commemorated on the St. Mary's War Memorial, Whitegate

The St. Mary's War Memorial, Whitegate

Dedicated to the Memory of James Southern

The brothers, James and Thomas Southern, both perished in the Great War. Thomas died in February 1917 at Ploegsteert in southern Belgium and James, just after hostilities ceased, in Salonica. A dedication to Thomas is included earlier in these pages. James and Thomas were the sons of Peter Henry and Elizabeth Southern who, in the years straddling the century, lived successively in Main Road and School Lane. Peter was a Marston man and earned his living as a Salt Boiler with one of the local Salt Companies.

James was born on 25 August 1892 and attended Moulton Council School. Aside from his brother Thomas, he had two sisters, Rachel and Elizabeth. Some years prior to the outbreak of war the family left Moulton to live in Weaver Street, Winsford. However, in the Electoral Rolls of 1914, Peter Henry is shown as having moved back to the village and living at 5 School Lane.

In June 1914 James married his sweetheart Mary Ann Weedall at Christ Church, Winsford. They then rented a house at 1 Done Fields, Wharton, Winsford and quickly produced two children, James Junior and William. It was from Done Fields that James enlisted in the Cheshire Regiment in 1916.

From June 1916, James served with the 2nd Battalion in Salonica and it was here, just after the Armistice, that he died of wounds in a British Hospital in Greece. He was 26-years old. Mikra cemetery, in which James lies, contains the graves of many soldiers who were brought in from other cemeteries in the locality.

It is extremely sad to record that on 5 December 1918 Mary Ann Southern completed a return to the Winsford Urban District Council. In it she records that her husband James is still serving in Salonica after 2 years 5 months. Three days after Mary submitted the report James was dead*.

*The return completed by Mary Ann Southern gives her husband's regiment as 'Labour Corps' and his Regimental number as 529446? It may well be that this was out-dated information or, alternatively, James may have been transferred to the Labour Corps sometime after his arrival in Salonica. In any case, his grave stone shows him in the 2nd Cheshire's.

Private James Southern

James Southern, Private No. 3/64818
2nd Battalion, The Cheshire Regiment
Died of wounds, Sunday, 8 December 1918. Age 26.
He is buried in Mikra British Cemetery, Kalamaria, Greece. 857

James Southern's headstone in Mikra British Cemetery, Kalamaria, Greece.

Private James Southern

James Southern's Awards

The British War Medal   The Victory Medal

Other memorials commemorating Private James Southern's name

In Sacred Memory
of
those connected
with this church and school,
who made the supreme sacrifice in the Great War
1914 – 1919.

Ashley Sam	Foster Jack	Ravenscroft Geo.
Buckley Robert	Groves Harry	Shaw Joseph
Buckley Robert H.	Hitchinson Horace	Southern James
Buckley Wilmot	Hodkinson Harry	Southern Thomas
Clarke Jervis	Lunt Willie	Tomlinson Dan.
Clarke William J.	Lunt George	Tomlinson Enoch
Cookson William H.	Maddock Jack	Tomlinson John
Crank John	Noden Arthur	Wakefield Peter
Didsbury Walter	Price Elijah	Weedon George

The memorial tablet in Moulton Methodist Church.

Christ Church War Memorial,
Wharton, Wimsford

Winsford Town War Memorial

Dedicated to the Memory of Dan Tomlinson

On an August day in 1918, Dan Tomlinson's only daughter Ethel, was given a little card to complete by her mother Florence. She planned to include it in the next letter or parcel to her husband. Sitting at the table with the card partially written, Ethel heard a knock at the door. Standing on the step of their little cottage was a telegraph boy…

Dan Tomlinson enlisted in the Cheshire Regiment at the beginning of hostilities. Before going to war he worked at Brunner and Monds alkali producing works at Lostock, Northwich. He was born on 19 April 1882 at 15 Chapel Street, Moulton. Married to Florence, they had three children Albert, Harold and Ethel.

On the 1881 Census Dan's parents William, a bricklayer, and Ann are shown as having three children, Agnes (13) Martha (7) and Edith (7 months). William's age is given as 37 and Ann's as 24. As Ann's age is confirmed on the 1891 Census (34) there is a mystery as to the parentage of Agnes and possibly Martha. An explanation is that Ann was William's second wife, or they could have been the children of relatives staying with them. The mystery deepens, for on the 1891 Census Agnes (who may well have married by then), Martha (17) and Edith (8) do not appear. However, Dan (8), Florence (6) and Albert (1) are recorded. At this time the family are living at 8 Chapel Lane, Moulton.

Before serving on the Western Front, Dan was with the Mediterranean Force. In a letter to Mr Winstanly of the Red Lion Hotel, he notes there was not much fighting, but what there was had been heavy. In the 1915 Parish and School Rolls of Honour, Dan is listed as serving with the 12th Cheshire's. He was promoted through the ranks until, in June 1917, he was commissioned as a Second-Lieutenant with The King's Liverpool Regiment.

On 10 August 1918, just three months before the end of the war, Dan was in trenches at Ayette, ten miles south of Arras, when a message needed to be delivered to the battalion on his flank. As his orderly was on other duties, he decided to walk the trench and deliver the communication himself. This was no big deal to Dan, for he had come up through the ranks and possibly, thought that he needed to stretch his legs anyway. It was the greatest mistake of his life. As he walked along the line he was sniped. He was rushed to the Casualty Clearing Station at Anzin-St Aubin were he succumbed to his wounds. Dan Tomlinson was 36-years old.

Second-Lieutenant Dan Tomlinson

Second-Lieutenant Dan Tomlinson
1st Battalion, The King's (Liverpool Regiment)
Killed in action, Saturday, 10 August 1918. Age 36.
His buried in Anzin-St. Aubin Cemetery, Pas de Calais, France. IV.D.24.

Second-Lieutenant Dan Tomlinson's headstone in Ansin-St. Aubin Cemetery
Pas de Calais, France.

Second-Lieutenant Dan Tomlinson

Dan Tomlinson's Award

The 1914–1915 Star   The British War Medal   The Victory Medal

Other memorials commemorating
Second-Lieutenant Dan Tomlinson's name

The memorial tablet in Moulton Methodist Church.

Second-Lieutenant Dan Tomlinson

Brunner Mond War Memorial, Winnington.

Brunner Mond War Memorial, Lostock.

Second-Lieutenant Dan Tomlinson

Then, Sergeant, later Second-Lieutenant, Dan Tomlinson with members of his family

Dedicated to the Memory of Peter Wakefield, M.M.

Peter Wakefield was a brave soldier who died on the Loos battlefield on 25 June 1918, aged 37. Prior to the outbreak of war he worked as a shiftman at Brunner Mond's Lostock works and lived with his wife Elizabeth and their eight children at Whortons Court, Northwich.

Peter was born in 1880 at 35 Regent Street, Moulton and is listed on the 1881 Census with his parents, Peter and Mary and their two daughters, Elizabeth (5) and Mary (3). By 1891, aged 11, he was living at 65 Regent Street with his Aunt and Uncle, Charles and Martha Such. Maybe by then, the small two-up and two-down terrace at No.35, had become too small for the expanding Wakefield family.

On 19 November 1914 Peter enlisted at Northwich and was posted to the 3rd Battalion, The East Lancashire Regiment at Fort Laira, Plymouth. After completing his training early in 1915, he was transferred to the regiment's 8th Battalion at Bournemouth. In March the battalion moved to Salisbury Plain to join the 112th Brigade, 37th Division. Shortly afterwards they were ordered to the Western Front and it was here, at Pozieres, in July 1916, on the killing fields of the Somme, that Peter's bravery was acknowledged by the award of the Military Medal.

At 9.20 am on 15 July 1916 the 8th Battalion assembled on the Contalmaison—La Boiselle road. A heavy mist lay over the ground heralding a bright warm Saturday. The unit was much below strength, owing to losses over previous days. As they advanced they were met by heavy machine gun and shell fire from Germans occupying the village of Pozieres. Men dropped like nine-pins until the remnants were forced to dig in around the Chalk Pit. They were reinforced by other units of the brigade and repulsed all attempts by the enemy to shift them. At 6.0 pm they again attempted to take the village with the same results. German machine gunners emerged from their deep dugouts to pour a devastating fire into the advancing men. Finally the Lancashire's dug in again, still 300-yards short of Pozieres. There they stayed until relieved at 2.30 am the following morning. In this action the 8th Battalion lost 365 casualties killed, wounded or missing.

In February 1917, in a letter to his wife, Sergeant Riley (Peter's brother-in-law also of the East Lancs.), asked her to tell Peter that: "He has got the Military Medal. It is in the 'Gazette', so it is all right". The citation reads:

For bravery in front of the enemy on 14/15th July 1916. With the aid of two other men he brought back a wounded comrade, under heavy fire, after he had dressed the mans wounds.

During this action at Pozieres, Peter was slightly wounded in the arm. In August 1916 he was discharged from the Army to work on essential munitions at Lostock*. Peter remained in his 'reserved occupation' until the spring of 1918 when he was recalled to his regiment's 1st Battalion serving in France.

On the night of 25 June 1918, the East Lancs. were positioned in front line trenches to the north of Bethune in the Floris subsector. Orders were received to the effect that 'D' Company were to carry out a night attack on the enemy line opposite. Object: 'To take prisoners for intelligence purposes'. Before going over the top Peter asked his friend to look after his epaulettes, cap badge, wallet and pocket book saying 'You never know what may happen'.

At 1 am two officers and 50 men of 'D' Company climbed out of their trenches and, under cover of a creeping barrage, assaulted the German trench system opposite. Enemy machine guns were neutralised and four prisoners taken. When the raiding party returned to their own trenches Peter Wakefield was not among those who answered their names at roll call. His body was never recovered and he is commemorated on the Loos Memorial to the missing at Pas de Calais. John Kipling, son of the poet Rudyard, and Fergus Bowes-Lyon, brother of the Queen Mother, are also listed on the same Memorial.

After the war Peter's wife Elizabeth re-married and became Mrs William (Bill) Gandy. The newly married couple and their ready-made family went to live in Barrymore Road, Weaverham, Northwich.

For some unaccountable reason Peter's name is not shown on Brunner Mond's Lostock or Winnington War Memorials. Neither is he listed on Moulton Council School's Roll of Honour.

*The Brunner Mond site at Lostock, Northwich manufactured Alkali products in huge quantities. Generally these were as lethal as a bag of flour. However, during the Great War modifications were made to the Ammonia Soda process there to enable part of the plant to produce Nitrate of Ammonia, an essential ingredient in the production of High Explosives.

Private Peter Wakefield, M.M.

Peter Wakefield, M.M., Private No. 17379
1st Battalion, The East Lancashire Regiment
Killed in action Tuesday, 25 June 1918. Age 37.
His name is commemorated on the Loos Memorial
Pas de Calais. France. Panel 65

The Loos Memorial, Pas de Calais, France.

Private Peter Wakefield, M.M.

Peter Wakefield's Award

The 1914 –1915 Star   The British War Medal   The Victory Medal

Other memorials commemorating Private Peter Wakefield's name

The Military Medal

Northwich Town War Memorial

The memorial tablet in
Moulton Methodist Church.

Dedicated to the Memory of Arthur Frederick Wilkinson

Arthur Wilkinson, born in Northwich in 1893, was the son of Frederick and Eliza Wilkinson.

He worked at the alkali producing factory of Brunner Mond & Company, Winnington. He enlisted at Chester in the 11th Battalion, the Cheshire Regiment. Just before he was drafted to the front, Arthur married his sweetheart, Annie, and they settled down to live at 26 Church Street, Moulton.

In the spring of 1917 Arthur was posted to his battalion, then serving on the Western Front. The 13th Battalion was involved in many battles including Messines in June and Third Ypres in July and August.

In March and early April 1918, during Ludendorff's operation 'Georgette' spring offensive, the 13th Battalion fought on the Somme at St. Quentin and Bapaume. Between 6 and 9 April, Albert found himself involved in the Battle of the River Lys and, on 20 April, he was killed in action. He was 26-years old.

His body was never recovered from the fields of Flanders and his name is now commemorated on the Tyne Cot Memorial to the Missing at Zonnebeke, Belgium, one of the 34,957 names of the fallen with no known grave. As recounted in Jack Maddock's dedication Tyne Cot Cemetery, is the largest of all Commonwealth War Grave Cemeteries with 11,856 burials, 101 special memorials and the Memorial records the names of 34,957 of the missing of the British Empire who fell in the Ypres Salient from 16 August 1917 to the end of the war, and who have no known graves.

Private Arthur Frederick Wilkinson

Arthur Frederick Wilkinson, Private No. 244767
11th Battalion, The Cheshire Regiment
Killed in action Sunday, 20 April 1918. Age 26.
His name is commemorated on the Tyne Cot Memorial to the Missing
Zonnebeke, West Flanders, Belgium. Panel 61 and 63.

The Tyne Cot Memorial to the Missing, Zonnebeke, West Flanders, Belgium

Private Arthur Frederick Wilkinson

Arthur Frederick Wilkinson's Awards

The 1914–1915 Star   The British War Medal   The Victory Medal

Private Arthur Frederick Wilkinson's name is also commorated on the
Brunner Mond Memorial, Winnington.

Brunner Mond War Memorial, Winnington.

Private Arthur Frederick Wilkinson

Arthur and his wife Annie, settled down to live at 26 Church Street, Moulton.

Field Marshal Haig leads British troops at the Victory Parade in Paris, in 1919

1919

AFTER THE STORM

T HERE IS LITTLE DOUBT that the 1919 Treaty of Versailles, signed in June between Germany and the Allies, laid the foundation for the Second World War. Germany was not only defeated in 1918 she was humiliated by the terms laid down in the treaty. They lost their colonies and also Alsace-Lorraine. Their fleet was reduced to a derisory 24 ships with no U-boats and they were instructed to pay full reparation for the war. The German people were consumed with hatred at what they considered to be a gross injustice. They were so incensed that only another war, in which they were the victors, would restore their pride and allow them to vent their anger on those who had asked, in their opinion, far too much. On 21 June in an act of defiance the skeletal naval crews on board the interned German Fleet in Scapa Flow opened the sea-cocks and sent their ships to the bottom of that huge natural harbour.

The forerunner of the United Nations Organisation. The League of Nations, was the world's first peacekeeping body. It was born at the Paris Peace Conference of 1919 and wrecked on the rocks of German resentment.

There are few reminders now of the devastation caused by the fighting on the Western Front. Some mine craters are preserved, as are token trench lines at Vimy Ridge, Beaumont Hamel and other spots along the old front line. Remains of The Citadel at Verdun, can be viewed by those with an interest in the French side of the conflict. The most abiding reminders of those four years of hell on earth, however, are the War Cemeteries and Memorials scattered, large and small, along the old static trench systems of France and Flanders. Each year when the fields are ploughed and raked in readiness for planting, the lines of the old trench systems show themselves to the pilgrims eye.

2,316 burial grounds are looked after by the Commonwealth War Graves Commission in France and Belgium alone. These places, where

Germans demonstrating in Berlin against the treaty provisions regarding Posen and Danzig

the shattered bodies of our men were put to rest, are immaculately kept and maintained by a the grateful nations. The ground in which they are interred, was given in pertetuity to Britain and the Commonwealth by our Allies. The missing are remembered on great Memorials such as those at Thiepval, Tyne Cot, Ploegsteert and, of course the Menin Gate at Ypres. Here at 8 oclock every evening throughout the year, buglers of the Ypres Fire Brigade, sound *Last Post* and *Reveille,* no matter what the weather or the audience – sometimes crowds, sometimes one or two passers-by.

Somewhere in the region of 7.5 million men died in the Great War – man's inhumanity to man knows no bounds, and is capable of the most dreadful carnage when bloodlust is on the agenda. The Spanish Flu of 1918–19 accounted for the deaths worldwide of between 20 and 40 million people – nature's inhumanity to man can be pretty awesome too.

Moulton

A memorial service was held at the Parish Church in January for Harry Groves, Horace Hitchinson, James Southern and Dan Tomlinson.

By early January, all the Moulton soldiers who had had the misfortune to fall into enemy hands and become prisoners-of-war, had returned to their homes. A 'Welcome Home' social and dance was held in the Verdin Institute to celebrate their release.

Of the eight ex-prisoners-of-war, one, Sergeant Archie Whitlow M.M. of the Royal Army Medical Corps, was reported in the Northwich Guardian to have died in captivity. The report of Archie's death is a complete mystery for, although he was a Moulton man he is not listed on any of the local War Memorials or Church Tablets. Neither the Commonwealth War Graves Commission nor the Royal Army Medical Corps in which he served with distinction, have any record of his having died in captivity, did he in fact survive? We may never know.

At the meeting of the committee of the Verdin Institute it was agreed that a full list of names of the men who had died should be compiled with a view to initiating a Verdin Institute Roll of Honour.

1919 was not a year without further grief for the village. The Spanish flu epidemic was reaping its deadly toll across Europe, and one of Moulton's returning soldier's, having spent three years fighting in some of the worst actions throughout Belgium and France, fell victim to this merciless sickness. On 24 February, **Arthur Noden** of the Machine Gun Corps, died of pneumonia brought on by the Spanish flu.

The Menin Gate, 1914

The Menin Gate, 1918

The Menin Gate Memorial, 1929

Dedicated to the Memory of Arthur Noden

Arthur Noden was a rebel at school and punished often for his sins. In the School Punishment Register of 1905 he is listed on four occasions: 1) for insubordination – 4 strokes; 2) for annoying the teacher – 5 strokes; 3) for disobedience and dirtiness – 2 strokes; 4) for bad work – 2 strokes. We will never know whether his parents, William and Mary, knew or whether he chose to suffer in silence for fear of a double dose of retribution from his Dad.

There is a record of Arthur's family living in Moulton Lane in the early 1880s. At that time there were two children: Thomas, aged 5 and Sarah Ann, aged 10 months. By 1891 the family, now totalling six, had moved to Kennerleys Lane. By the end of the decade they had moved once more, this time to Chapel Street.

Arthur was born on 8 July 1893 and at 4 to 5 years of age attended the village Council School. We know that he married Minnie Whitlow prior to, or just after, the outbreak of war and that they set up house at 54 Regent Street and had two children.

When war was declared, Arthur enlisted in the 10th Battalion, The Cheshire Regiment and went to France in late 1915 or early 1916. In mid-1915 he was listed on the village and school Rolls of Honour as serving in the 10th Cheshire's. In a letter to his mother in June 1916, Arthur's brother Harry, said that he had met up with his brothers George and Arthur for the first time in 18 months.

In late 1916 Arthur was trained and proficient in the use of the Vickers-Maxim machine gun and joined one of the 7th Brigade's Machine Gun Companies. During 1916, Arthur saw action with either the infantry or the Machine Gun Corps in the Somme Battles of Albert, Bazentin Ridge, Pozieres Ridge, Mouquet Farm, Ancre Height, Stuff Redoubt and Regina Trench. In 1917 the 25th Division fought at Messines and at Third Ypres (Passchendaele). 1918 saw Arthur involved in the fighting that pushed back the Germans back before their final capitulation in November.

Tragically, after fighting through France and Belgium for over three years, Arthur Noden returned home only to die within days of pneumonia brought on by Spanish Flu. He was buried at St.Wilfrid's, Davenham on 1 March 1919 with full military honours, his coffin draped with the Union Flag. The Reverend J T Vale conducted the service at the graveside.

In later years Arthur's wife Minnie re-married, became Mrs Bennett and went to live at 1 Oak Street, Northwich.

Private Arthur Noden

Arthur Noden, Private No. 72524
The Machine Gun Corps (Inf.)
He died at home on Monday, 24 February 1919. Age 25.
He is buried in Davenham (St. Wilfrid) Churchyard. New 659

Arthur Noden's headstone in Davenham (St. Wilfrid) Churchyard.

Private Arthur Noden

Arthur Nolan's Awards

The 1914–1915 Star   The British War Medal   The Victory Medal

Other memorials commemorating Private Arthur Nolden's name

In Sacred Memory
of
those connected
with this church and school,
who made the supreme sacrifice in the Great War
1914–1919.

ASHLEY SAM	FOSTER JACK	RAVENSCROFT GEO.
BUCKLEY ROBERT	GROVES HARRY	SHAW JOSEPH
BUCKLEY ROBERT H.	HITCHINSON HORACE	SOUTHERN JAMES
BUCKLEY WILMOT	HOOKINSON HARRY	SOUTHERN THOMAS
CLARKE JERVIS	LUNT WILLIE	TOMLINSON DAN.
CLARKE WILLIAM J.	LUNT GEORGE	TOMLINSON ENOCH
COOKSON WILLIAM H.	MADDOCK JACK	TOMLINSON JOHN
CRANK JOHN	NODEN ARTHUR	WAKEFIELD PETER
DIDSBURY WALTER	PRICE ELIJAH	WEEDON GEORGE

The memorial tablet in Moulton Methodist Church.

Private Arthur Noden

Northwich Town War Memorial

Tyne Cot Military Cemetery

Unresolved Mysteries

Dᴜʀɪɴɢ ᴛʜᴇ ᴄᴏᴜʀꜱᴇ of this research, and despite countless enquiries, the histories of three men remain a mystery. Their names and as much detail as is known about them are recorded here. They deserve nothing less.

Alfred Barber

Alfred Barber is commemorated on the village War Memorial and the Parish Church Tablet. No other definitive information is available.

A total of 52 'A. Barbers' are listed on the CD Rom 'Soldiers Died 1914 – 1918', none appear to have any connection with either Moulton or Northwich. Crewe – yes, Lymm – yes, but not Moulton. Strangely, Alfred is not mentioned in the local press at any time during the period of the war and there are no records of him having attended the local Council School. In the 1919 Electoral Rolls for Moulton Village the name Barber does not appear.

It can only be assumed that sometime after the war ended, but before the Memorial and Church Tablet were finalised, either his wife or his parents came to live in the locality and submitted his name for inclusion on the Memorial and Church Tablet.

Ernest Blythe

Again, Ernest Blythe is commemorated on the village War Memorial and on the Parish Church Tablet. No other unquestionable proof relating to his connection with Moulton can be found.

There are five E. Blyth's recorded by the Commonwealth War Graves Commission as having died in the Great War. None show a connection with Moulton Village. Three were born in the North West of England at Birkenhead, Helsby and Runcorn.

The 1881 census records a family group named Bailey living in Main

Street, Frodsham, Cheshire. Living with them was a widower John Blythe and two children Julia F Blythe aged six and Ernest Blythe aged five. If this is 'our' Ernest Blythe then he would have been about 38-years of age in 1914 – possible but unlikely. In the Moulton Council School records held in the Cheshire Records Office mention is made on 13th September 1918 of a teacher, Mrs Blythe, who was 'absent by permission'. She may well have been the mourning widow of Ernest.

As with Alfred Barber the relatives of Ernest Blythe may have moved to Moulton towards the end of the war and submitted his name for inclusion on the Memorials.

Srgeant Archie Whitlow, M.M.

In a report in the Northwich Guardian of 17 January 1919 mention is made that Sergeant Archie Whitlow had died in captivity whilst a prisoner of the Germans. Strange, therefore, that he is not commemorated on any of the memorials in the locality, neither, does the Commonwealth War Graves Commission register or The Soldiers Died in 1914 – 1918 CD make any reference to his death.

Archie was born in 1891 and attended Moulton Council School. On leaving school he worked in Knutsford and whilst there joined the St. Johns Ambulance Brigade. He was a very fine athlete and was well known in mid-Cheshire for his running ability. He belonged to both Northwich and Crewe Harriers.

At the very start of the war, Archie enrolled in the Army and was posted to the Royal Army Medical Corps were his St. Johns training would prove invaluable. For the first year he served in hospitals throughout the UK and by July 1915, when his name appears on the Parish Roll of Honour, he had been promoted to Lance-Corporal.

In early September 1915 he married Phoebe Brooks of Weaver Street, Winsford at Over Parish Church. Ann Whitlow was Phoebe's bridesmaid. Prior to the wedding Archie, who was 26-years old, lived with his parents at 10 Main Road, Moulton. Shortly after the wedding Archie received orders to embark for France.

Just before Christmas 1915 Archie wrote to the teachers and scholars of his old school to thank them for their very welcome gift of a parcel of 'goodies'. He went on to say that he had very pleasant memories of his school days and that he would visit them when next he came home on leave.

Unresolved Mysteries

In June 1916 under the heading 'Moulton Casualties' Archie (by now a full Corporal), in a letter home, mentions that he had treated some of his old pals from the village including Lance-Corporal Walker and Bob Buckley. In November, in a letter to Mr Bowker, his old headmaster, he describes some of the sights he has seen and the 'queer' places he has visited. On one occasion, he said, a shell had exploded only feet away from him, but, by some miracle, had left him unscathed. Again he recounted meeting lads from the village and talking with them. The weather, he said, was atrocious with rain day after day and seas of mud everywhere.

Despite the war Archie was still running and keeping himself fit. During a break from front line duty he led an RAMC team to victory in a local sports competition.

Sometime in the summer of 1917 Corporal Archie Whitlow was awarded the Military Medal for 'Bravery and devotion to duty' for rescuing wounded soldiers from the battlefield. In September he came home on leave and visited both teachers and scholars at his old school. He proudly wore his M.M. for all to see and was presented with a gift by Mr Bowker who said that Corporal Whitlow had brought honour to himself, the village of Moulton and to his old school. Archie received a great reception from the assembled gathering.

This is the last record of Archie Whitlow until the report of his death in captivity in January 1919. Why such a brave son of Moulton is not recorded on the memorial or church tablets is a mystery. The reason may be forever lost in the mists of time. Did he really die or did the Northwich Guardian get it wrong in their report? Did he turn up later? Were the details of his death unrecorded or lost in the confusion after the war? Did Phoebe, his widow, move away from the district and have his name recorded on some distant memorial?

Author's note: If any reader can throw any light on these three soldiers, corrections will be made to any subsequent re-prints of this dedication.

The Cross of Sacrifice, or Great Cross, stands in every British Military Cemetery

Moulton expatriates who also died

IN ADDITION TO the 34 servicemen listed on the village War Memorial and Church Tablets, ten other Moulton ex-patriots perished in the war. Nine of the 10 were born in the village, but all ten had moved away prior to the outbreak of hostilities. They too are remembered in this dedication:

Private Percy Bell, 12th Battalion, The Cheshire Regiment.

Percy Bell was born in Moulton in 1895 and after leaving school he worked for Northwich Council. He was one of five brothers who responded to the call to arms. He enlisted at Northwich, joining the 12th Cheshires. He was the son of Henry and Ann Bell who were living at 9 Chapel Street, Castle, Northwich at the time of his death. The fortunes of his four serving brothers were mixed. Harry, died of wounds in January 1916 whilst serving with the Kings Liverpool Regiment. Arthur and Earnest, both of the 2nd Battalion, Cheshires, were made prisoners of war and saw out the duration in captivity in Germany. Thomas served throughout the conflict with the King's Liverpool Regiment.

On 29 October 1916, whilst serving with his battalion in Macedonia, Percy, who was at that time an officer's orderly, was last seen looking for his officer in trenches which his battalion had attacked and over-run. He was never seen again and his body was never recovered. Percy was 21 years old and his name is inscribed on the Doiran Memorial, Greece. He is also commemorated on the Northwich Town Memorial in Church Walk.

Private Herbert Hampton
1st Battalion The Cheshire Regiment.

Little is known about Herbert Hampton. He was born in Moulton and, at some point, left the village. On the 1891 Census a family named Hampton is recorded as living at 31 Main Road. Charles, the father (34) and his wife Charlotte (32), had three children at the time -Gertrude (5), Charles (4) and Mabel (1). Charles' name is on the 1914 Electoral Rolls, living at the time in 30 Regent Street. He would then be about 27-years old. He may well have married a local girl and settled in the village when the rest of the family moved away.

Herbert was drafted to the 1st Battalion, the Cheshire Regiment. He died three days before the end of the war on 8 November 1918. His remains are interred in Cologne Southern Cemetery, Germany – Grave V. G. 4. This fact would seem to indicate that he died in captivity. It is known that more than 1,000 Allied prisoners of war were buried there.

Private John Hollins Hitchinson
6th Battalion, The South Lancashire Regiment.

John was amongst the thousands killed in action on the Gallipoli peninsula in the campaign of 1915. His body was never recovered and he is commemorated on the Helles Memorial, Turkey – Panels 139 and 140. The memorial is in the form of an obelisk some 30 metres high and can be seen by ships entering the Dardanelles *en route* to Istanbul.

At the time of his death, on 10 August 1915, John's parents, Fred and Emily Hitchinson were living in Derby Road, Farnworth, Widnes. Their son, who was living in Moulton in 1896, was 19 when he was killed. He enlisted at Warrington in the 6th Battalion, South Lancashire Regiment and posted to the front soon after his training was finished. John may well have been a relation of Horace Hitchinson who died in India in October 1918 and whose name is mentioned earlier.

Private (acting Lance-Corporal) William Lunt
10th Battalion The Lancashire Fusiliers.

Willie Lunt was the elder of two brothers killed in the Great War. Born in Moulton in April 1891, he lived with his parents at 11 Regent Street before leaving the village to live at Cledford, Middlewich, He attended Moulton Council School and, on leaving, obtained a job with the Winsford Co-op Society before joining the Maypole Dairy Company in Manchester.

In November 1914 Willie enlisted in the 10th Battalion, the Lancashire Fusiliers. His first taste of battle was at Sulva Bay in the Dardanelles in June 1915. He was wounded in the leg and thigh on the Western Front in November 1916 and hospitalised to Brackley in Northamptonshire. On his recovery he returned to the Western Front in February 1917.

On 13 September 1918, two months before the end of the war, he wrote to his father saying he was expecting leave in the very near future. Five days later, on Wednesday 18 September, his battalion attacked Gouzeaucourt, to the west of Cambrai. Immediately after the attack Willie was detailed to repair a broken signal wire when a shell exploded behind him – death was instantaneous. He was 27-years old.

He lies in Gouzeaucourt New British Cemetery, Nord, France – Grave 1V. G. 5. His name is commemorated on the Middlewich Town War Memorial and the Moulton Methodist Church Tablet.

Private George T Lunt
1/1st Battalion King's Shropshire Light Infantry

George Lunt was the younger brother of Willie Lunt and was born 17 September 1896. He lived with his parents 11 Regent Street, Moulton until they moved to 21 Booth Lane, Cledford, Middlewich during the early 1900s. He attended Moulton Council School in his early years and later Middlewich Council School. After leaving school he worked for Messrs Verdin Cook and Company and in his leisure time became quite an accomplished dancer with Mrs Swain's dancing troupe. He excelled in Spanish and Irish dancing and had a very keen sense of humour.

Aged 17, he managed to persuade the recruiting sergeants at Winsford into believing he was 19 and was accepted into the Cheshire Regiment. Recruiting Sergeants were renowned for accepting under-age recruits when trying to fulfil their quotas. The much-repeated tale of asking a young lad to go for a walk around the block and to think again about his age was a regular feature of the recruiting sergeant's armoury.

In 1915 George was posted to Gallipoli, were his brother Willie was fighting with the Lancashire Fusiliers (they never managed to get together there). George contracted an enteric disease and was shipped back to hospital in Birmingham, staying there for four months. In October 1916 he was declared fit again for active service and posted to the Egyptian front. Aged 20, he was killed in action there on 6 November 1917 .

George Lunt is buried in Beersheba War Cemetery, Israel – Grave E.36. His name, and that of his brother Willie, is inscribed on Middlewich Town War Memorial and also on the Moulton Methodist Church Tablet. At the time of his death his father, John, was a widower, Sophie, his wife, having died some time before.

Private George W Lyon
1/5th Battalion, TheDurham Light Infantry.

George Lyon was born at 77, Regent Street, Moulton. His father William, was a Coppersmith. Sometime before the war the family moved to Greatham, Stockton-on-Tees were George met and married his wife Mary. They settled in Greatham before George enlisted in the 5th Battalion, The Durham Light Infantry at the outbreak of war.

During the Battle of the Lys in April 1918, the battalion were attacked by German infantry advancing along the railway line to capture Le Sart, a mile west of Merville in France. During this action George was killed. He was 27-years old and is buried in Aval Wood Military Cemetery, Vieux-Berquin, Nord, France. Grave III. C. 5.

Private William Poole
1st Battalion, The King's Shropshire Light Infantry.

There is little information on William Poole who was born in Moulton At the outset of the war he lived in Crewe and enlisted at Shrewsbury in the 1st Battalion, King's Shropshire Light Infantry. He was killed in action on 18 September 1916 during the assaults on Flers-Courcelette.

Sergeant Charles Price, 11th Battalion, The Cheshire Regiment.

At 4.30 pm on the afternoon of Sunday 16. January1916 a 'stray' bullet took the life of Charles Price in the Ypres Salient. He was 39-years old and left a wife, Annie and a daughter living at 51 James Street, Northwich.

Charlie Price was born at 78 Regent Street, Moulton and is recorded on the 1881 Census as aged two, living with his parents Henry and Ann. At some time after leaving Moulton with his parents to live at 29, James Street, Northwich, Charles joined the army as regular soldier, served in India and was then placed onto the reserve sometime before the commencement of hostilities in 1914. He then secured a job at the Ammonia Soda Companies Works at Plumley, Northwich.

When war broke out, despite the fact that his period as a reservist had expired, he volunteered and was drafted to the 11th Battalion, The Cheshire Regiment. His service experience saw him quickly promoted to Sergeant and, due to a shortage of officers, he commanded No. 9 Platoon of his battalion from when it left England to the time of his death in January 1916. Just before he was killed his wife received a letter saying he was looking forward to a period of leave and to spending time with her and their daughter. He rests in the London Rifle Brigades Cemetery at Ploegsteert, Belgium. Grave II.A.22. His is also commemorated on the Northwich Town Memorial, Church Walk, Northwich.

Private Elijah Price
2nd Battalion, The South Lancashire Regiment.

Elijah Price was born in Runcorn on 9 January 1885. Towards the end of the 1880s, Elijah's parents, Alfred and Elizabeth, moved to Moulton village. In 1891 the family settled at 19 Main Road, Moulton. Alfred's occupation is given as 'Barber' on the Census return. Just prior to living in Main Road, the family lived for a little while at 5 Church Street.

On leaving school Elijah worked for a Mr Burston, a farmer, of King Street before joining Messrs Sanders and Handley, millers of Northwich, where he worked six years before enlisting in the 2nd Battalion, The South Lancashire Regiment. By this time his father had died and Elijah with his invalided mother had moved to 44 Bond Street, Winnington.

Having served at the front for 12 months Elijah, was killed in action in the Ypres Salient on 29 April 1918. His body was never recovered and his name is commemorated on the Tyne Cot Memorial, panels 92, 93 and 162A. His name does not appear on the Moulton viillage War Memorial although it is shown on the Moulton Methodist Church Tablet. The name E. Price appears on the Northwich Town War Memorial in Church Walk.

Elijah had two married brothers. At the time of his death one had been discharged and the other was still serving abroad. His mother was incapacitated, and may well have lived with one of her married sons in Moulton, submitted Elijah's name there for inclusion on the Moulton Methodist Church Tablet.

Private George Vallender
7th Battalion, The King's Shropshire Light Infantry.

George Vallender was 24-years of age when he died of wounds in a Casualty Clearing Station some 20 kilometres behind the Somme front line on 16 July 1916. The son of William and Phoebe Vallender, he was born at 45 Main Road, Moulton. At some point the family moved to 9 Esther Street, Widnes from where George was drafted into the 7th Battalion, King's Shropshire Light Infantry, having enlisted at Warrington. He is buried in the Corbie Communal Cemetery Extension, Somme, France. Grave I.D.37.

The memorial plaque reads:

In Sacred Memory
of
those connected
with this church and school,
who made the supreme sacrifice in the Great War
1914 – 1919.

Ashley Sam	Foster Jack	Ravenscroft Ged.
Buckley Robert	Groves Harry	Shaw Joseph
Buckley Robert H.	Hitchinson Horace	Southern James
Buckley Wilmot	Hodkinson Harry	Southern Thomas
Clarke Jervis	Lunt Willie	Tomlinson Dan.
Clarke William J.	Lunt George	Tomlinson Enoch
Cookson William H.	Maddock Jack	Tomlinson John
Crank John	Moden Arthur	Wakefield Peter
Didsbury Walter	Price Elijah	Weedon George

Memorials, Tablets and Rolls Of Honour

ALTHOUGH ALL 34 MEN from the village who died in Great War are commemorated on the village war memorial and Parish Church Tablet, some appear on other memorials around the district. Acting Petty Officer William Cookson, for instance, is remembered on no less than six Memorials throughout the locality. One explanation is that men, on marrying, moved away from the village to live in other areas. Their parents, on the other hand, remained in Moulton and subsequently submitted their names for inclusion on the Moulton memorial. Large employers such as Brunner Mond Ltd. and Salt Union Ltd erected memorials to their dead employees. In other instances, and this may be the answer to the lack of information on Alfred Barber and Ernest Blythe, parents and/or wives of men who had died, may have moved into the village after their deaths and then submitted their names for inclusion on the Moulton memorial and Church Tablets. It is significant that neither of the two men mentioned are listed on the Methodist Church Tablet that only lists 'those connected with this church and Sunday school.

Northwich Town War Memorial, Church Walk, Northwich.

Amongst the names on the memorial are:

> J Clarke
> W H Cookson
> W Didsbury
> A Noden
> W Pool *
> C Price *
> E Price **
> P Wakefield

Born in Moulton but resident in Northwich at time of death. Names not listed on Moulton village War Memorial.

**Name listed on Moulton Methodist Tablet but not on village War Memorial.*

Winsford Town War Memorial, Town Square, Winsford

Amongst the names on the memorial are:

F J Bates
W H Cookson
G Greatbanks
J Shaw
J Southern
T Southern
J Tomlinson

Brunner Mond War Memorials, Winnington and Lostock

To the Glorious Memory of the Men Employed by Brunner Mond and Co. Ltd who fell during the Great War August 1914–June 1919

Amongst the names on the memorials are:

Robert Buckley
Jervis Clarke
George Greatbanks
Horace Hitchenson
Harry Hodkinson
Albert Victor Walker
Arthur Frederick Wilkinson
Dan Tomlinson (Lostock)

Salt Union War Memorial

To the glory of God and in memory of those men from the Winsford Works of the Salt Union Ltd who gave their lives in the Great War 1914–1918 Erected by their fellow work people 1925

Amongst the names on the memorial are:

H Groves
G Ravenscroft
J Shaw
T Southern
E Tomlinson
J Tomlinson

St. Chads War Memorial, Over, Winsford

Amongst the names on these memorials are:

Private James Fred Bates
Corporal Arnold Buckley
Leading Seaman William H Cookson
Private Joseph Shaw
Ptrivate Thomas Southern
Lance-Corporal John Tomlinson

Memorials, Tablets And Rolls Of Honour

Christ Church War Memorial, Wharton, Winsford

Amongst the names on these memorials are:

Fred Bates

Arnold Buckley

James Southern

St Mary's War Memorial, Whitegate, Winsford

Amongst the names on these memorials are:

Pte John Tomlinson

Pte Oliver Middleton

Moulton Methodist Church. Church Tablet

*In Sacred Memory of those connected with this Church and School
who made the Supreme Sacrifice in the Great War 1914 – 1918*

Ashley Sam	Foster Jack	Ravenscroft Geo
Buckley Robert	Groves Harry	Shaw Joseph
Buckley Robert H	Hitchinson Horace	Southern James
Buckley Wilmot	Hodkinson Harry	Southern Thomas
Clarke Jervis	Lunt Willie *	Tomlinson Dan
Clarke William J	Lunt George *	Tomlinson Enoch
Cookson William H	Maddock Jack	Tomlinson John
Crank John	Noden Arthur	Wakefield Peter
Didsbury Walter	Price Elijah *	Weedon George

*Not listed on Village War Memorial or Parish Church Tablet

Roll Of Honour

*Messrs Brunner Mond and Company Limited list of Employees who served in
H M Forces In the Great War 1914–1918 for King and Country. April 1920*

Joined H M Forces	2688
Returned	790
Died	291
Honours	67

Amongst the names within the Roll of Honour booklet are:

Winnington

Buckley Robert, Pte	10th Cheshire's	Died
Clarke Jervis, Pte	7th East Lancs	Killed In action
Greatbanks George, Pte	2nd Cheshire's	Killed In action
Hitchinson Horace, Pte	8th Cheshire's	Died
Hodkinson Harold, Pte	3rd Cheshire's	Died
Walker Albert V, Pte	10th Cheshire's	Died
Wilkinson Arthur F, Pte	11th Cheshire's	Presumed dead

Lostock

Tomlinson Dan, Lt	1st Kings L'pool	Killed in Action

*Note: Above details from Brunner Mond's Roll of Honour booklet in the Public Records Office,
Duke Street, Chester.*

Roll Of Honour

The Salt Union and Subsidiary Companies
The Great War 1914 – 1918

Number who joined the forces 1169
Died   174
Gained Honours   22

Amongst those listed under Cheshire are:

> Pte. H Groves, 9th Cheshire's
> Pte. G Ravenscroft, 8th North Lancs.
> Pte. J Shaw, 14th Cheshire's
> Pte. T Southern, 14th Cheshire's
> Gunner E Tomlinson, RGA
> Pte. J Tomlinson, 4th Durham Light Infantry

Note:
1) All of the above are listed on Salt Union's Memorial Tablet at Winsford. There is a picture of this Tablet at the County Records Office, Duke Street, Chester.
2) The Roll of Honour can also be found in the County Records Office, Duke Street, Chester.

Facts, data and comment

THE FIRST SHOT fired by a British soldier during the Great War was on the morning of 22 August 1914. It was a sunny day when Sergeant E Thomas, M.M., 'C' Squadron, 4th Royal Irish Dragoon Guards, took up position under trees on the Mons–Charleroi road. Suddenly a scout reported a troop of Uhlans (German Light Cavalry) advancing at a leisurely pace down the road, the officer leading, smoking a cigar. Suddenly the Germans saw their enemy and turned to flee back along the road. The Irish Dragoons gave chase, scattering the Uhlans in all directions. The order was then given for 4th troop to take dismounted action. Immediately Sergeant Thomas spotted a mounted German cavalry officer some 400 yards away, he took careful aim and fired. The officer fell from his horse either dead or wounded.

Statistics relating to total losses during the Great War change dependant on which reference book is consulted. The following data is as reliable as any:

Deaths

Central Powers:		Allies:	
Germany:	1,800,000	Russia:	1,700,000
Austro/Hungary:	922,000	France:	1,300,000
Turkey:	325,000	U.K.:	888,000
Bulgaria and others:	93,000	Italy:	400,000
		Rumania	335,000
		USA:	50,500
		India:	72,000
		Australia:	62,000
		Canada:	65,000
		Serbia:	45,000
		Belgium:	44,000
		New Zealand:	18,000
		Others:	20,000
Central Powers Total: 3.140, 000		**Allies Total:**	4,999,500

Total Dead – All Forces: 8,139,500

The best estimate of civilian deaths in all theatres is 8,750,000 millions. Just a shade over those killed in uniform.

A staggering 70% (500,000) British soldiers who gave their lives in the war were under 30 years of age. Of the millions who enlisted a total of 80% survived to tell their tales of the horrors of modern warfare. They would tell them of gas, mines and machine guns, trenches and mud, pain and fear and finally of their good fortune in having survived.

Throughout the war the proportion of junior officers killed in relation to other ranks was marginally greater. However, in 1916 the chances of any officer being killed was twice that of other ranks. For example, when the 1st Battalion, Hampshire Regiment attacked on 1 July 1916 (The first day of the Somme) they lost every one of their officers.

The first battle deaths of the Great War were recorded when *HMS Amphion* was struck by a mine on 6 August 1914 and several sailors were lost.

The first Army death occurred in West Africa – Private Bai of the Gold Coast Regiment died on 15 August 1914.

The first British Army officer to perish in action was Lieutenant George Masterman Thompson, 1st Battalion, Royal Scots and Gold Coast Regiment on 22 August 1914.

The first allied soldier to die in action on the Western Front was Private John Parr, 4th Battalion, Middlesex Regiment. He was killed at Mons on Friday 21 August 1914.

Ironically, the last man to die in action was also killed at Mons at 11.0 am on Monday 11 November 1918. He was a Canadian, Private George Lawrence Price, aged 25, 28th Battalion, Canadian Infantry. No doubt thinking that hostilities had ceased, he showed himself to a German sniper, who, in a moment of sheer vindictiveness, took aim, pulled the trigger and needlessly ended the life of a brave man. It is hoped that this German soldier carried the remorse of this, his last action, through to the end of his life. Both men are buried in St. Symphorien Military Cemetery, Mons, Belgium.

It is believed that the youngest soldier to die in the war was John Condon, 2nd Royal Irish Regiment. He was born at Waterford, Ireland in June 1901 and joined the local militia in 1913, giving his age as 16 years. He progressed from the militia and joined the 3rd Battalion, The Irish Regiment at Clonmel, County Tipperary in 1914. He was killed in action at Mouse Trap Farm, Ypres in May 1915. John Condon was just one month short of his 14th birthday.

At the other end of the scale the oldest serviceman to die in a war zone was Lieutenant Henry Webber, 7th Battalion, The South Lancashire Regiment and died on 21 July 1916, aged 68. Lieutenant Webber was a native of Horley in Surry and for 40 years was a member of the London Stock Exchange. He was mentioned in despatches and is buried in Dartmoor Cemetery on the Somme.

It is popular today amongst some members of the media and writing fraternity, to de-bunk anything and everything relating to the past. particularly the British Generals of the Great War. Field Marshal Sir Douglas Haig, a favourite target, is vilified and portrayed as a butcher who gave no thought for his men as he despatched them to their deaths. According to these commentators the General Staff spent their time living a life of luxury in their Château's behind the line and away from any danger. Their men, on the other hand, were made to live in abject misery in their forward positions. Do we really believe that the prosecution of any war, involving millions of men and armaments can to be organised by staff officers standing in front line trenches up to their knees in mud? Senior officers did lead their battalions into action, Generals were killed as they met with the troops and their officers in the front line. In Martin Middlebrook's excellent book *The first day on the Somme* he lists 53 senior officer casualties on the first day. Of these 31 were killed and 22 wounded. Most were Lieutenant-Colonels who were either killed or wounded leading their men over the top. Two were Brigadier Generals. Great Britain lost 888,000 men in the conflict, Germany 1,800,000 Russia 1,700,000 France 1,300,000, Austro/Hungary 922,000 and Italy 600,000. So which armies were led by bad Generals?

Most senior historians believe that Haig did all that he could, given the circumstances and equipment at the time. After all, our only means of mobility across open country, until the tank was introduced in 1917, was the horse. Mistakes were made of course, but in the end we won and Haig's brilliant plan to achieve victory in 1918 is very often 'conveniently' forgotten! It must be said that this much maligned Field Marshall was well regarded by both his men and their officers. After the war he worked tirelessly to promote the Earl Haig Poppy Fund which to this day is a source of help to the wounded of all wars.

Of the 170,000 British servicemen taken prisoner in the Great War a total of 20,000 died in captivity. Large numbers died of wounds, but 12,000, unforgivably, died of starvation. They were made to work in mines, chemical plants and on the land. They were very often ill-treated and sometimes shot. The 1929 Geneva Convention signed by the majority of civilised nations, but not by Russia or Japan, would attempt to safeguard the basic human rights of prisoners-of-war in future wars of the 20th century. In the 1939-45 conflict Germany, to a degree, treated prisoners better than most. However, there were atrocities and the best remembered of these was the execution of 50 Allied prisoners after their 'Great Escape' from Stalag Luft III, the notorious camp so well portrayed in the film of that name.

As the British Tommy settled down to life in the trenches he would, with a pinch of nostalgia, christen the trenches with names that reminded him of home –Blighty Valley, Essex Street, Manchester Alley, Sausage Valley etc.

Place names in France and Belgium often created problems for the lads, who often had difficulty in getting their tongues around the strange, unfamiliar names. The simple solution was to anglicise the names. Consequently Ypres became *Wipers*, Mouquet Farm – *Mucky Farm*, Ploegsteert – *Plugstreet*, Wyschaete – *Whitesheet* etc. They also gave their own descriptive names to certain points – Shrapnel Corner, Salvation Corner, Suicide Road, Hellfire Corner, International Corner, Belgian Battery Corner and the like. Strongpoints, battalion headquarters, supply dumps, roads and tracks were also nicknamed by the troops, invariably related to their regiments or home towns – Rifle House, Somerset House, Lancashire Farm, Bunhill Row, The Strand, Leinster House, Gordon Farm, and so on. They also had their pet names for the German shells and mortars that rained down upon them. Small calibre, high velocity artillery shells that whizzed as they approached and exploded with a large bang became 'Whizzbangs'. Larger calibre shells were known as 'Willies', 'Black Marias', 'Crumps' or 'Woolly Bears'. One large calibre shell was nicknamed a 'Jack Johnson' after a black boxer of the day – this shell on bursting emitted a cloud of black acrid smoke. A large trench mortar (Minenwerfer) was a 'Flying Pig' or 'Coal Box' which could be seen in flight, and hopefully avoided.

One man, who had the foresight at the very beginning of the war, to foresee the enormity of the task of recording the locations of the graves of men who had died in battle was Sir Fabian Ware, later Director-General of Graves Registration and Enquiries. He convinced the authorities that the work should start immediately and this was agreed. Originally working as commander of the Mobile Unit, British Red Cross Society, then the Graves Registration Commission (formed in 1915). This eventually became the Imperial War Graves Commission in 1917 which, after the war, became the Commonwealth War Graves Commission that to this day looks after British British Commonwealth Military Cemeteries all over the world. Anyone who has ever visited one of these cemeteries will applaud the way they are tended and looked after by a very special and dedicated staff.

At the very outset it was decided that headstones would be plain with no distinction made on account of rank, race or creed. A standard inscription would show the regimental badge, followed by the deceased number, name, rank, regiment, date of death, age and religious symbol (Christian Cross, Star of David etc.). If the next-of-kin wished, they could subscribe to a personal

Facts, data and comment

inscription at the foot of the headstone. Costs just after the war were 3.5d per letter up to a maximum of 66 letters or spaces. In today's values this equates to 30p per letter or say, £20 for a full inscription. A bit thick when the family had already forfeited their loved one in the cause of freedom.

The Telegram

Wives, parents and loved ones with men on active service, learned to dread the sight of their postman and, even more so, the telegraph boy. Very often they were the harbingers of terrible news. After the commencement of the Somme offensive on 1 July 1916, when Kitchener's New Army battalions were decimated by machine gun fire from the German trenches, telegrams and letters of condolence fell like autumn leaves on the towns and villages of the United Kingdom.

An example of the carnage that befell one battalion says it all. When the whistles blew at 7.30 am on that fateful day, the men of the 10th Battalion, West Yorkshire Regiment climbed from their trenches and advanced towards the German wire. In two hours, 710 Yorkshiremen from that battalion were lying, either dead or wounded in No-Man's Land.

Other battalions suffered similarly on that day, in fact, over 30 battalions lost over 500 men from their total compliment of approximately 1,000.

Moulton Village Statistics

Most of the following data is based on information gleaned from publications circulated during, or after the war. It is not definitive, but merely an indication to help the reader understand the magnificent contribution made by Moulton Village towards the war effort:

Total village population:	circa. 1100
Served in the armed forces:	230 (20% of the village population)
Total died:	34 (15% of those who enlisted or 3% of the village population)
Killed in action:	20*
Died of wounds/sickness:	12*
Wounded:	100+ (Based on a 3:1 ratio of those who died)
First to die:	John Crank – 30 October 1914
Last to die:	Arthur Noden – 24 February 1919 (Influenza)
Died furthest afield:	Horace Hitchinson – India
Died together:	Wilmot Buckley and George Greatbanks on 3 October 1915

Died at home:	John Crank, Harry Hodkinson, Arthur Noden – all three are buried in Davenham Cemetery:
Youngest to die:	Sam Ashley, Jack Maddock and Peter Wakefield – all 19 years old.
Oldest to die:	Robert Buckley – 39 years of age.
Highest rank:	Second-Lieutenant Dan Tomlinson
Number with graves:	15*
Number without graves:	17*

Names recorded on Memorials.
Missing from these statistics: Alfred Barber and Ernest Blythe.

In Which They Served

The Regiments in which the 34 Men of Moulton served:

Regiment	Number
The Cheshire Regiment	16
The Durham Light Infantry	1
The East Lancashire Regiment	1
The Kings (Liverpool Regiment)	2
The Loyal North Lancashire Regiment	1
The Machine Gun Corps (Infantry)	1
The Manchester Regiment	2
The Royal Army Service Corps	2
The Royal Field Artillery and Royal Horse Artillery	1
The Royal Fleet Reserve	1
The Royal Welsh Fusiliers	1
Prince Albert's (Somerset Light Infantry)	1
The Prince of Wales Volunteers (South Lancashire Regiment)	2
Total	**32**

Note: The Regiments of Alfred Barber and Ernest Blythe are unknown.

Medals

Medals or 'Gongs', awarded the 34 ranged from the the 1914 Star (the 'Mons' Star awarded to all who served in France and Belgium between 5 Aug. and 10 Nov. 1914), the 1914–1915 Star (Awarded to all who served between 5 Aug.and 31 Dec. 1915) – no man could hold both 'Stars – the British War Medal, the Victory Medal and the Military Medal (an award for bravery). Every man who served automatically received two or three medals. The first three (including one of the 'Stars') would become sardonically known as Pip, Squeak and Wilfred by the returning troops. Those who received only the British War and Victory Medal (men who did not serve in 1914) wore Mutton and Jeff. These names were derived from cartoon characters of the time, which generally summed-up what the troops thought of the medals.

I

BIBLIOGRAPHY

50th Anniversary Souvenir Brochure of The Battle of the Somme: Arras & District British Legion
A Centenary History 1894–1994: Robert Galley
A Cheshire Parish at war: Ann Clayton
A Short History of World War 1: Brig.Gen. Sir James A Edmonds
Battlefield guide to the Somme: Major & Mrs Holt
British battalions on the Somme: Roy Westlake
Courage Remembered: Major Edwin Gibson M.B.E. and G Kingsley Wood. H.M.S.O. 1989.
Dear Mrs Jones: Mark Potts & Joy Bratherton
Domesday Book St
History of The First World War: Sir Basil Liddell Hart
Monuments of War: Colin McIntyre. Robert Hale, 1990.
Of those who lie in Foreign Fields: R L Stanley & Joy Bratherton
One day on the Somme: Barry Cuttell
Regimental Histories and Battalion War Diaries relating to the 34 men.
Salient Points Two: Tony Spagnoly & Ted Smith. Pen & Sword
Silent Witnesses: Herbert Fairlie Wood and John Swettenham. Hekkert, Toronto. 1974.
The Anatomy of a Raid: Tony Spagnoly & Ted Smith. Pen & Sword 1988.
The Big Push: Brian Gardner. Cassell, 1961.
The British Army of 1914: Major R Money Barnes. Seeley Service & Co Ltd., 1968.
The First Day on the Somme: Martin Middlebrook. W. W. Norton Inc., 1972
The Great War: John Terraine
The Immortal Heritage: Fabian Ware. Cambridge University Press, 1937.
The Last Year: Wilfred Owen
The Silent Cities: Sidney C Hurst P.A.S.I.: Methuen & Co Ltd., 1929.
The Unending Vigil: Philip Longworth. Constable & Co Ltd., 1967.
The Winsford Returns: Alan Ravenscroft – 1996
The World War One Source Book, P J Haythornthwaite. Arms and Armour Press, 1992.
World War 1: Peter Simkins

Other

Absentee Voters Lists – Northwich Division: Cheshire County Council Records Office.
Electoral Rolls – Northwich Division
Moulton Council School Records
Northwich Guardian & Northwich Chronical – 1914–1921: Northwich Library
Salt Union Ltd Roll Of Honour
St.Stephen's Parish Magazines 1919 – 1923
St Stephen's Vestry Minutes 1917–1924
The Moulton Verdin Institute's Minute Book 1916–1920
Trade Directories
United Alkali Ltd Roll Of Honour
Winsford Guardian – 1914–1921: Winsford Library
Private Papers, Ted Smith

INDEX

R

Rains, Mr and Mrs –31
Ravenscroft, George –1, 89
Ravenstone Dale, –127
Rawlinson, General –49,122
Red Lion –31, 52
Red Lion's Soldiers and Sailors
Patriotic Fund –89, 127
Regent Street –3, 8, 9, 11, 53, 89,
196-198
Rifle House –208
River Aisne –17
River Lys –121, 198
River Marne –17
River Meuse –48
River Scarpe –85
River Somme –48
River Weaver –9

S

Salt Boiler –11
Salt Union Ltd –3, 11, 201
Salvation Corner –208
Sanders, Reverend Canon –7
Sarajevo –15
Sausage Valley –208
Scapa-Flow –181
Scherpenberg –121
Schlieffen plan –17
Sea of Marmara –29
Second Battle of Ypres –26
Second Passchendaele –85
Second World War –181
Scheer, Admiral Reinhard –47
Shannon, George –13
Shaw, Joseph –1, 53
Shrapnel Corner –208
Soldiers and Sailors Christmas
Comforts Fund –127
Soldiers Christmas Cheer Fund –31
Somerset House, –208
Somme –18, 85, 123, 199
Southern, Private James –127
Southern, James –1, 183
Southern, Thomas –1, 89
Spanish flu –122, 183
St. Johns Ambulance Bgd –192

St. Julian –27
St. Quentin –121
St. Yves –85
St. Eloi –26
Stockall, Albert –13
Suez Canal –29
Suicide Road –208
Sulva Bay –29, 196

T

Tannenberg –19
Taylor, W –53
The Caucasus –52
The Citadel at Verdun –181
The League of Nations –181
The Lion –9
The Manor of Bostock and Davenham –12
The Strand –208
Thiepval –183
Third Battle of Ypres –85, 87
Thomas, Sergeant E, M.M. –205
Togoland –19
Tomlinson, Dan –1, 183, 210
Tomlinson, Enoch –1, 89
Tomlinson, John –1
Tomlinson, Mr J J –53
Tomlinson, Second-Lieutenant Dan –127
Travellers Rest –9, 31
Treaty of Versailles –181
Trentino –52
Trotski –87
Turner, Reverend J C and Mrs –127
Tyne Cot –183

U

U-boat –83, 89, 121, 125
United Nations Organisation –181

V

Vale, Reverend J T –7, 127
Vallender, Private George –199
Vallender, William and Phoebe –199
Verdin Institute –3, 9, 31, 89, 127, 183
Verdin, Sir Joseph –89
Verdun –47, 48, 123
Villers-Bretonneux –122
Vimy Ridge –27, 85, 181

W

Wakefield, Peter –1, 210
Wakefield, Private Peter –1
Walker, Lance-Corporal –193
Walker, Albert V –1
Walker, Albert –89
Ware, Sir Fabian –206
Warrington –196, 199
Waterford, Ireland –206
Weaver Street, Winsford –192
Webber, Lieutenant Henry –206
Weedon, George –1, 31
West Flanders –18
Western Front –18
Whitby –19
Whitesheet –208
Whitlow, Ann –192
Whitlow, Archie –53, 193
Whitlow, Sergeant Archie, M.M.
–183, 192
Whizzbangs –208
Widnes –3
Wilkinson, Arthur F –1
Wilkinson, Private Arthur
Frederick –127
Willies –208
Wilson, President –83
Winnington New Stars Pierrot
Troop –127
Winsford –9, 52, 197
Winsford Guardian –53
Winstanly, Mr J –31, 53, 127
Wipers –208
Woolly Bears –208
Wright, Frederick –13
Wyschaete –208

Y

Yardley, Joseph –1, 51, 53
Youth Group Headquarters –9
Ypres –18, 122, 208
Ypres Fire Brigade –18, 183
Ypres Salient –18, 26, 85, 198, 199

Z

Zeebrugge –18, 89, 125